TEEN RIGHTS AND FREEDOMS

| Self-Incrimination

TEEN RIGHTS AND FREEDOMS

I Self-Incrimination

Noël Merino
Book Editor

GREENHAVEN PRESS
A part of Gale, Cengage Learning

Stevens Memorial Library
20 Memorial Dr.
Ashburnham, MA 01430
978-827-4115

GALE
CENGAGE Learning·

Detroit • New York • San Francisco • New Haven, Conn • Waterville, Maine • London

Elizabeth Des Chenes, *Director, Content Strategy*
Cynthia Sanner, *Publisher*
Douglas Dentino, *Manager, New Product*

© 2014 Greenhaven Press, a part of Gale, Cengage Learning

WCN: 01-100-101

Gale and Greenhaven Press are registered trademarks used herein under license.

For more information, contact:
Greenhaven Press
27500 Drake Rd.
Farmington Hills, MI 48331-3535
Or you can visit our Internet site at gale.cengage.com.

ALL RIGHTS RESERVED
No part of this work covered by the copyright herein may be reproduced, transmitted, stored, or used in any form or by any means graphic, electronic, or mechanical, including but not limited to photocopying, recording, scanning, digitizing, taping, Web distribution, information networks, or information storage and retrieval systems, except as permitted under Section 107 or 108 of the 1976 United States Copyright Act, without the prior written permission of the publisher.

For product information and technology assistance, contact us at:

Gale Customer Support, 1-800-877-4253.
For permission to use material from this text or product, submit all requests online at www.cengage.com/permissions.

Further permissions questions can be emailed to permissionrequest@cengage.com.

Articles in Greenhaven Press anthologies are often edited for length to meet page requirements. In addition, original titles of these works are changed to clearly present the main thesis and to explicitly indicate the author's opinion. Every effort is made to ensure the Greenhaven Press accurately reflects the original intent of the authors. Every effort has been made to trace the owners of copyrighted material.

Cover Image © ruigsantos/Shutterstock.com.

LIBRARY OF CONGRESS CATALOGING-IN-PUBLICATION DATA

Self-incrimination / edited by Noël Merino.
   p. cm. -- (Teen rights and freedoms)
   Includes bibliographical references and index.
   ISBN 978-0-7377-6432-1 (hardback)
   1. Self-incrimination--United States I. Merino, Noël, editor of compilation.
   KF9668.S45 2014
   345.73'056--dc23
                        2013036415

3817900073540
Apple 8/14

Printed in the United States of America
1 2 3 4 5 6 7 18 17 16 15 14

Contents

Foreword

*"In the truest sense freedom cannot be
bestowed, it must be achieved."*
Franklin D. Roosevelt,
September 16, 1936

The notion of children and teens having rights is a relatively recent development. Early in American history, the head of the household—nearly always the father—exercised complete control over the children in the family. Children were legally considered to be the property of their parents. Over time, this view changed, as society began to acknowledge that children have rights independent of their parents, and that the law should protect young people from exploitation. By the early twentieth century, more and more social reformers focused on the welfare of children, and over the ensuing decades advocates worked to protect them from harm in the workplace, to secure public education for all, and to guarantee fair treatment for youths in the criminal justice system. Throughout the twentieth century, rights for children and teens—and restrictions on those rights—were established by Congress and reinforced by the courts. Today's courts are still defining and clarifying the rights and freedoms of young people, sometimes expanding those rights and sometimes limiting them. Some teen rights are outside the scope of public law and remain in the realm of the family, while still others are determined by school policies.

Each volume in the Teen Rights and Freedoms series focuses on a different right or freedom and offers an anthology of key essays and articles on that right or freedom and the responsibilities that come with it. Material within each volume is drawn from a diverse selection of primary and secondary sources— journals, magazines, newspapers, nonfiction books, organization newsletters, position papers, speeches, and government documents, with a particular emphasis on Supreme Court and lower court decisions. Volumes also include first-person narratives from young people and others involved in teen rights issues, such as parents and educators. The material is selected and arranged to highlight all the major social and legal controversies relating to the right or freedom under discussion. Each selection is preceded by an introduction that provides context and background. In many cases, the essays point to the difference between adult and teen rights, and why this difference exists.

Many of the volumes cover rights guaranteed under the Bill of Rights and how these rights are interpreted and protected in regard to children and teens, including freedom of speech, freedom of the press, due process, and religious rights. The scope of the series also encompasses rights or freedoms, whether real or perceived, relating to the school environment, such as electronic devices, dress, Internet policies, and privacy. Some volumes focus on the home environment, including topics such as parental control and sexuality.

Numerous features are included in each volume of Teen Rights and Freedoms:

- An annotated **table of contents** provides a brief summary of each essay in the volume and highlights court decisions and personal narratives.
- An **introduction** specific to the volume topic gives context for the right or freedom and its impact on daily life.
- A brief **chronology** offers important dates associated with the right or freedom, including landmark court cases.
- **Primary sources**—including personal narratives and court decisions—are among the varied selections in the anthology.
- **Illustrations**—including photographs, charts, graphs, tables, statistics, and maps—are closely tied to the text and chosen to help readers understand key points or concepts.

- An annotated list of **organizations to contact** presents sources of additional information on the topic.
- A **for further reading** section offers a bibliography of books, periodical articles, and Internet sources for further research.
- A comprehensive subject **index** provides access to key people, places, events, and subjects cited in the text.

Each volume of Teen Rights and Freedoms delves deeply into the issues most relevant to the lives of teens: their own rights, freedoms, and responsibilities. With the help of this series, students and other readers can explore from many angles the evolution and current expression of rights both historic and contemporary.

Introduction

The self-incrimination clause of the Fifth Amendment to the US Constitution guarantees, "No person . . . shall be compelled in any criminal case to be a witness against himself." This right to avoid self-incrimination is a right that most people are familiar with because of its frequent reference in pop culture. This right guaranteed under the Fifth Amendment is often referenced in television shows and movies where criminal defendants "plead the Fifth," meaning that they invoke their Fifth Amendment privilege against self-incrimination. Most people can recount from memory a portion of what is known as the *Miranda* warning that informs criminal suspects of the rights against self-incrimination: "You have the right to remain silent. Anything you say can and will be used against you in a court of law." Yet people may not be aware of the reason for the right to avoid self-incrimination and what it actually means.

The right to avoid self-incrimination stems from a concern about the fair administration of criminal justice. The purpose of the self-incrimination clause is to guarantee that government may not compel a confession from a suspect through coercion or force. The protection applies whether the suspect is at trial or questioned prior to trial. This protection forces the government to focus on evidence to make its case, rather than relying on a confession.

The US Supreme Court's decision in *Miranda v. Arizona* (1966) forever changed the way in which the self-incrimination clause is understood. That decision put in place a requirement that when law enforcement takes any suspect into custody, the suspect must be informed of his or her rights. The wording does not have to be the same in every case, but law enforcement must clearly inform a suspect of the following four guarantees prior to any questioning: that the suspect has the right to remain silent, that anything the suspect says can be used against him or her in a court of law, that the suspect has the right to the presence of an attorney, and that if he or she cannot afford an attorney one will be appointed prior to any questioning if he or she so desires. If law enforcement fails to inform a suspect who is in custody of his or her *Miranda* rights and proceeds with questioning, any evidence discovered during that questioning will not be admissible at trial. However, if a suspect waives his or her right to remain silent, questioning may proceed and any evidence discovered will be allowed at trial.

Juveniles have the same rights as adults under the self-incrimination clause. Thus, any juvenile who is taken into custody for questioning must be given a *Miranda* warning. The Supreme Court has determined that the age of a suspect is often relevant to determining whether or not the suspect perceives to be in custody. Thus, law enforcement may have different requirements for informing suspects of their *Miranda* rights depending on whether the suspect is an adult or a juvenile. Most recently, in 2011, the court held that the questioning by police of a thirteen-year-old at school could very well amount to the determination that the boy was in custody. The mandatory nature of school and the perception by teenagers of the authority of adults at school was all seen as relevant to determining whether a juvenile should be given *Miranda* warnings in an effort to protect against self-incrimination.

The privilege against self-incrimination guaranteed by the Fifth Amendment is an important component of the Bill of Rights. The way in which the privilege has been interpreted over the years, however, is not without controversy. Some charge that the right to avoid self-incrimination has gone too far and that the *Miranda* decision has resulted not in greater constitutional protections for suspects but in more criminals avoiding conviction. However, there are opinions just as strong in support of *Miranda*, and some even say that the right of criminal suspects to avoid self-incrimination still is not protected adequately, especially for juveniles. A variety of viewpoints on the Fifth Amendment's privilege against self-incrimination—through court decisions, analysis by experts, and personal commentary—is explored in *Teen Rights and Freedoms: Self-Incrimination.*

Chronology

1791   The Bill of Rights is adopted by the United States, guaranteeing a right against self-incrimination in the Fifth Amendment: "No person . . . shall be compelled in any criminal case to be a witness against himself."

1868   The Fourteenth Amendment to the US Constitution is adopted, wherein its due process clause guarantees that the Bill of Rights apply to the states as well as the federal government: "Nor shall any State deprive any person of life, liberty, or property, without due process of law."

1936   In *Brown v. Mississippi* the US Supreme Court rules that physical punishment or torture may not be used to compel a confession to a crime.

1948   In *Haley v. Ohio* the Supreme Court rules that it is a violation of the due process clause of the Fourteenth Amendment to hold a juvenile suspect in secret custody in order to secure a coerced confession.

1962   In *Gallegos v. Colorado* the Supreme Court determines that the age and maturity of a suspect have a direct bearing on determining whether a confession is voluntary.

1966   In *Miranda v. Arizona* the Supreme Court rules that confession to a crime is inadmissible in court if the suspect has not been informed by law enforcement of his or her privilege against self-incrimination, which becomes known as the *Miranda* warning.

1967   In *In re Gault* the Supreme Court determines that juveniles who are charged with delinquency have the right to notification of criminal charges, the right to counsel, the right to confront witnesses, and the privilege against self-incrimination.

1977   In *Oregon v. Mathiason* the Supreme Court determines that *Miranda* warnings are not required when law enforcement questions a suspect who is not in custody.

2000   In *Dickerson v. United States* the Supreme Court upheld the requirement that law enforcement inform criminal suspects of their *Miranda* rights, striking down a law enacted by Congress that undermined such a requirement.

2004   In *Yarborough v. Alvarado* the Supreme Court determines that age is not a relevant factor in determining whether someone is in custody and, therefore, should be informed of *Miranda* rights.

2010   In *Florida v. Powell* the Supreme Court holds that although all suspects in custody must be informed of their *Miranda* rights, the wording that law enforcement can use to convey those rights can vary.

2010   In *Berghuis v. Thompkins* the Supreme Court rules that criminal suspects must explicitly invoke the right to remain silent for the protection against self-incrimination to apply.

2011   In *J.D.B. v. North Carolina* the Supreme Court rules that age is a relevant factor in determining whether someone is in custody and, therefore, should be informed of *Miranda* rights, thereby overruling its decision in *Yarborough v. Alvarado.*

> *"The concept of 'taking the Fifth' has resonance for nearly every American familiar with the prohibition against government-compelled self-incrimination."*

The Fifth Amendment Protects Against Self-Incrimination

Stephen Stetson

In the following viewpoint, Stephen Stetson discusses the wide-ranging content of the Fifth Amendment to the US Constitution, noting that it guarantees five distinct liberties, one of which is the right to avoid self-incrimination. Stetson contends that the self-incrimination clause of the Fifth Amendment was written into the Bill of Rights following the British legal tradition. He claims the right evolved and expanded over the years, with the US Supreme Court's decision in Miranda v. Arizona *in 1966 drastically expanding protections against self-incrimination. Stetson concludes that the rights identified in* Miranda *have come to be some of the most well-known by the general public. Stetson is a policy analyst for Arise Citizens' Policy Project in Alabama.*

The Fifth Amendment to the Constitution of the United States is a wide-ranging and variously interpreted part of the Bill

Stephen Stetson, "The Fifth Amendment," *Encyclopedia of the Supreme Court of the United States*, David S. Tanenhaus, ed. Detroit: Macmillan Reference, vol. 2, 2008, pp. 212, 216–217. Copyright © 2012 by Cengage Learning. All rights reserved. Reproduced by permission.

of Rights. The Amendment is often described in terms of five relatively separate sections, each covering a separate freedom or liberty, and each with its own history of litigation, interpretation, and application.

The Fifth Amendment

Ratified by the states in 1791, the Fifth Amendment establishes the right of an accused person to a grand jury under certain circumstances, the right to be free from repeated prosecutions and punishments for a single offense, the right to due process of law, the right to avoid self-incrimination, and the right to receive due compensation for government takings of private property. The Fifth Amendment reads:

> No person shall be held to answer for a capital, or otherwise infamous crime, unless on a presentment or indictment of a Grand Jury, except in cases arising in the land or naval forces, or in the Militia, when in actual service in time of War or public danger; nor shall any person be subject for the same offense to be twice put in jeopardy of life or limb; nor shall be compelled in any criminal case to be a witness against himself, nor be deprived of life, liberty, or property, without due process of law; nor shall private property be taken for public use, without just compensation.

The Fifth Amendment is notable both for the incredible diversity of cases in which it is invoked—from the nuances of criminal procedure to disputes involving the right to abortion—and also for its unique position in the popular imagination. In a manner distinguishing it from virtually every other constitutional amendment, the concept of "taking the Fifth" has resonance for nearly every American familiar with the prohibition against government-compelled self-incrimination. The amendment is invoked by name in innumerable trials, hearings, depositions, and interrogations, for it provides a series of protections for individuals, running from pretrial indictment through the

A police officer displays a Miranda *warning card.* Miranda v. Arizona *(1966) stipulated that police officers must provide the accused with specific warnings upon arrest.* © Robert Houston/ AP Images.

trial itself, as well as protections for property. It is one of the central bulwarks against government impositions on individuals. . . .

The History of the Self-Incrimination Clause

The self-incrimination portion of the Fifth Amendment is inexorably linked in the minds of an entire generation with the anticommunist witch hunts of the so-called McCarthy era. The House Un-American Activities Committee was created in 1938, but it did not fully begin to propel the Fifth Amendment to the forefront of the American consciousness until after World War II, when it issued a string of subpoenas and held hearings seeking out communists and communist sympathizers.

The evolution of the privilege to "take the Fifth," predates the Cold War. Unlike other parts of the Fifth Amendment, the prohibition on self-incrimination did not stem from Magna Carta.

In fact, the barons compelling legal reforms from the sovereign were not particularly concerned about self-incrimination, nor was compelled self-incrimination particularly widespread at that time. Rather, the forces influencing the development of the privilege developed as European legal systems moved toward jury trials and inquisition, and as the importance of evidence collection, including that collected from the accused, increased substantially.

As Church courts developed and employed so-called *inquisitio* proceedings—which acted simultaneously as accuser, prosecutor, judge, and jury—protests began to occur about the use of oaths and interrogations to compel testimony. Nonetheless, civil law began to copy ecclesiastical procedures, including anonymous accusations and secret proceedings. An opposition to the use of sworn oaths followed both the Church's persecution of "heretics" and the state's persecution of "traitors."

In 1583 Elizabeth, Queen of England, created what would be known as the High Commission, designed in part to ferret out the religious dissent of Catholics and Puritans. Inquisitorial oaths (and imprisonment for failure to swear them) were pervasive prosecutorial techniques. Although the common law courts tried to check the power of the ecclesiastical courts, the use of oaths continued up through the trial of John Lilburne, who was arrested in 1637 for trafficking in seditious books. After an epic legal struggle, Lilburne's opposition to the self-incriminating oaths helped precipitate the abolishment by Parliament in 1641 of the High Commission and the controversial Star Chamber courts. At the same time, the administration of oaths by the ecclesiastical courts was forbidden. In Lilburne's 1649 trial, the court appeared to accept the notion that it could not compel answers to incriminatory questions. Although judges in subsequent years would continue to attempt to pressure suspects into self-incrimination, the immunity from compelled self-incriminatory testimony was thus established in British legal tradition, and it was ultimately exported, if sporadically, to the colonies.

George Mason (1725–1792) wrote the privilege against self-incrimination into the Virginia Declaration of Rights in 1776, and other states followed by including the privilege in their own bills of rights. In 1789 James Madison and the First Congress cemented the privilege into the Bill of Rights with relatively no discussion or debate.

The Evolution of the Privilege Against Self-Incrimination

Once embedded in the Fifth Amendment, the privilege against self-incrimination evolved and expanded from merely forbidding a penalty of contempt of court when an accused refuses to answer incriminatory questions at trial. For example, in *Blau v. United States*, (1950) the Supreme Court held that a witness is entitled to claim the privilege when answering questions that might elicit answers supplying even "a link in the chain of evidence" in the government's case against the witness. Significantly, a defendant's refusal to testify may not be taken as a sign of guilt.

Two cases decided on the same day in 1964 further expanded on the so-called "right to remain silent." In *Malloy v. Hogan*, (1964) the Supreme Court held, for the first time ever, that the Fifth Amendment's protection against self-incrimination applies to the states through the due process clause of the Fourteenth Amendment. In *Murphy v. Waterfront Commission*, decided the same day as *Malloy*, the main question before the Court was whether a state government may force a witness to answer questions under an immunity statute when those answers might also prove incriminating under federal law. Having established in *Malloy* that the states are bound by the self-incrimination clause, the Court went on to say that incriminating testimony compelled by one government cannot be used by another. Thus, federal prosecutors would be prohibited from making any use, direct or derivative, of state-compelled incriminating testimony.

The Right Against Self-Incrimination

The Fifth Amendment's right against self-incrimination permits an individual to refuse to disclose information that could be used against him or her in a criminal prosecution. The purpose of this right is to inhibit the government from compelling a confession through force, coercion, or deception. The self-incrimination clause applies to any state or federal legal proceeding, whether it is civil, criminal, administrative, or judicial in nature. This privilege is frequently invoked during the trial phase of legal proceedings, where individuals are placed under oath and asked questions on the witness stand.

The privilege is also asserted with some frequency during the pretrial phase of legal proceedings. In the pretrial phase of criminal cases, it is usually asserted in response to pointed questions asked by law enforcement agents, prosecutors, and other government officials who are seeking to determine the persons responsible for a particular crime. During the pretrial phase of civil cases, parties may assert the right against self-incrimination when potentially damaging questions are posed in depositions and interrogatories.

"Fifth Amendment," Gale Encyclopedia of American Law, *third ed., vol. 4, ed. Donna Batten. Detroit: Gale, 2010, pp. 436–442.*

Justice Arthur Goldberg, writing for the Court in *Murphy*, outlined the long list of policy reasons for the privilege:

It reflects many of our fundamental values and most noble aspirations: our unwillingness to subject those suspected of crime to the cruel trilemma of self-accusation, perjury or contempt; our preference for an accusatorial rather than inquisitorial system of criminal justice; our fear that self-incriminating statements will be elicited by inhumane treatment and abuses;

our sense of fair play which dictates a "fair state-individual balance by requiring the government to leave the individual alone until good cause is shown for disturbing him and by requiring the government in its contest with the individual to shoulder the entire load; our respect for the inviolability of the human personality and of the right of each individual "to a private enclave where he may lead a private life"; our distrust of self-deprecatory statements; and our realization that the privilege, while sometimes "a shelter to the guilty," is often "a protection to the innocent." (internal citations omitted)

The Historic *Miranda* Decision

These cases set the table for *Miranda v. Arizona*, (1966), one of the most well-known and controversial Supreme Court decisions of the twentieth century. Whereas a considerable amount of the scholarship before 1966 involved the use of the self-incrimination clause during anticommunist dragnets and other interrogations, the Court's holding in *Miranda* inaugurated a seismic shift in the world of Fifth Amendment jurisprudence. The *Miranda* decision extended broad new protections to the accused and placed new requirements on the practices of law enforcement officers.

Miranda is perhaps the most cited Supreme Court case of all time, with nearly verbatim quotes from the decision appearing in countless television crime dramas and other popular culture representations of policing and interrogations. The enduring legacy of *Miranda* is not only the extension of the Fifth Amendment's prohibition against self-incrimination into the public's consciousness of a "right to remain silent," it is also the requirement that, at some point, law enforcement officials must verbalize the adversarial nature of their relationship with the accused. If warnings are not properly given, statements made during interrogations may be excluded at trial. This requirement was immediately controversial, although it has become less so over time. When *Miranda* was decided, however, many observers were outraged that a suspect's incriminating statements could be suppressed simply because police had not verbally communicated to the suspect his or her Fifth Amendment rights.

> *"The Fourteenth Amendment prohibits the police from using the private, secret custody of either man or child as a device for wringing confessions from them."*

Juveniles Have Due Process Rights That Disallow Coercive Confessions

The Supreme Court's Decision

William O. Douglas

In the following viewpoint, William O. Douglas, writing for a plurality of the US Supreme Court, contends that the due process rights guaranteed by the Fourteenth Amendment prohibit law enforcement from using coercive methods for obtaining a confession from a suspect. Douglas argues that the methods used to extract a confession to a crime from a fifteen-year-old boy violated his due process rights. Douglas claims that juveniles are particularly susceptible to coercion, requiring law enforcement to take extra caution in guaranteeing younger suspects due process. Douglas is the longest-serving justice in the history of Supreme Court, nominated by President Franklin D. Roosevelt and serving from 1939 to 1975.

Petitioner was convicted in an Ohio court of murder in the first degree and sentenced to life imprisonment. The Court

William O. Douglas, Plurality Opinion, *Haley v. Ohio*, US Supreme Court, January 12, 1948.

of Appeals of Ohio sustained the judgment of conviction over the objection that the admission of petitioner's confession at the trial violated the Fourteenth Amendment of the Constitution. The Ohio Supreme Court, being of the view that no debatable constitutional question was presented, dismissed the appeal. The case is here on a petition for a *writ of certiorari* [review] which we granted because we had doubts whether the ruling of the court below could be squared with *Chambers v. Florida* [1940], *Malinski v. New York* [1945], and like cases in this Court.

Confessing to the Crime

A confectionery store was robbed near midnight on October 14, 1945, and William Karam, its owner, was shot. It was the prosecutor's theory, supported by some evidence which it is unnecessary for us to relate, that petitioner, a Negro boy age 15, and two others, Willie Lowder, age 16, and Al Parks, age 17, committed the crime, petitioner acting as a lookout. Five days later—around midnight October 19, 1945—petitioner was arrested at his home and taken to police headquarters.

There is some contrariety in the testimony as to what then transpired. There is evidence that he was beaten. He took the stand and so testified. His mother testified that the clothes he wore when arrested, which were exchanged two days later for clean ones she brought to the jail, were torn and blood-stained. She also testified that, when she first saw him five days after his arrest he was bruised and skinned. The police testified to the contrary on this entire line of testimony. So we put to one side the controverted evidence. Taking only the undisputed testimony, we have the following sequence of events. Beginning shortly after midnight, this 15-year old lad was questioned by the police for about five hours. Five or six of the police questioned him in relays of one or two each. During this time, no friend or counsel of the boy was present. Around 5 A.M.—after being shown alleged confessions of Lowder and Parks—the boy confessed. A confession was typed in question and answer form by the police.

At no time was this boy advised of his right to counsel, but the written confession started off with the following statement:

"We want to inform you of your constitutional rights, the law gives you the right to make this statement or not as you see fit. It is made with the understanding that it may be used at a trial in court either for or against you or anyone else involved in this crime with you, of your own free will and accord, you are under no force or duress or compulsion and no promises are being made to you at this time whatsoever."

"Do you still desire to make this statement and tell the truth after having had the above clause read to you?"

"A. Yes."

He was put in jail about 6 or 6:30 A.M. on Saturday, the 20th, shortly after the confession was signed. Between then and Tuesday, the 23rd, he was held incommunicado. A lawyer retained by his mother tried to see him twice, but was refused admission by the police. His mother was not allowed to see him until Thursday, the 25th. But a newspaper photographer was allowed to see him and take his picture in the early morning hours of the 20th, right after he had confessed. He was not taken before a magistrate and formally charged with a crime until the 23d—three days after the confession was signed.

The trial court, after a preliminary hearing on the voluntary character of the confession, allowed it to be admitted in evidence over petitioner's objection that it violated his rights under the Fourteenth Amendment. The court instructed the jury to disregard the confession if it found that he did not make the confession voluntarily and of his free will.

The Methods Used to Obtain the Confession

But the ruling of the trial court and the finding of the jury on the voluntary character of the confession do not foreclose the independent examination which it is our duty to make here. If the undisputed evidence suggests that force or coercion was used to

Section One of the Fourteenth Amendment to the US Constitution

All persons born or naturalized in the United States, and subject to the jurisdiction thereof, are citizens of the United States and of the state wherein they reside. No state shall make or enforce any law which shall abridge the privileges or immunities of citizens of the United States; nor shall any state deprive any person of life, liberty, or property, without due process of law; nor deny to any person within its jurisdiction the equal protection of the laws.

exact the confession, we will not permit the judgment of conviction to stand even though, without the confession, there might have been sufficient evidence for submission to the jury.

We do not think the methods used in obtaining this confession can be squared with that due process of law which the Fourteenth Amendment commands.

What transpired would make us pause for careful inquiry if a mature man were involved. And when, as here, a mere child—an easy victim of the law—is before us, special care in scrutinizing the record must be used. Age 15 is a tender and difficult age for a boy of any race. He cannot be judged by the more exacting standards of maturity. That which would leave a man cold and unimpressed can overawe and overwhelm a lad in his early teens. This is the period of great instability which the crisis of adolescence produces. A 15-year old lad, questioned through the dead of night by relays of police, is a ready victim of the inquisition. Mature men possibly might stand the ordeal from midnight to 5 A.M. But we cannot believe that a lad of tender years is a match for the police in such a contest. He needs counsel and support if he is not to become the victim first of fear, then of panic. He needs someone on whom to lean lest the overpowering presence

In Haley v. Ohio (1948), the US Supreme Court argued that juveniles are particularly susceptible to coercion from law enforcement officials. The court ruled that law enforcement is required to take extra caution in guaranteeing younger suspects due process. © Robert Nickelserg/Getty Images.

of the law, as he knows it, may not crush him. No friend stood at the side of this 15-year old boy as the police, working in relays, questioned him hour after hour, from midnight until dawn. No lawyer stood guard to make sure that the police went so far and no farther, to see to it that they stopped short of the point where he became the victim of coercion. No counsel or friend was called during the critical hours of questioning. A photographer was admitted once this lad broke and confessed. But not even a gesture towards getting a lawyer for him was ever made.

This disregard of the standards of decency is underlined by the fact that he was kept incommunicado for over three days during which the lawyer retained to represent him twice tried to see him and twice was refused admission. A photographer was admitted at once; but his closest friend—his mother—was not allowed to see him for over five days after his arrest. It is said that these events are not germane to the present problem because they happened after the confession was made. But they show such a callous attitude of the police towards the safeguards which respect for ordinary standards of human relationships compels that we take with a grain of salt their present apologia that the five-hour grilling of this boy was conducted in a fair and dispassionate manner. When the police are so unmindful of these basic standards of conduct in their public dealings, their secret treatment of a 15-year old boy behind closed doors in the dead of night becomes darkly suspicious.

The Constitutional Requirements of Due Process

The age of petitioner, the hours when he was grilled, the duration of his quizzing, the fact that he had no friend or counsel to advise him, [and] the callous attitude of the police towards his rights combine to convince us that this was a confession wrung from a child by means which the law should not sanction. Neither man nor child can be allowed to stand condemned by methods which flout constitutional requirements of due process of law.

But we are told that this boy was advised of his constitutional rights before he signed the confession and that, knowing them, he nevertheless confessed. That assumes, however, that a boy of fifteen, without aid of counsel, would have a full appreciation of that advice, and that, on the facts of this record, he had a freedom of choice. We cannot indulge those assumptions. Moreover, we cannot give any weight to recitals which merely formalize constitutional requirements. Formulas of respect for constitutional safeguards cannot prevail over the facts of life which contradict them. They may not become a cloak for inquisitorial practices and make an empty form of the due process of law for which free men fought and died to obtain.

The course we followed in *Chambers v. Florida, White v. Texas* [1940], *Ashcraft v. Tennessee* [1944], and *Malinski v. New York*, must be followed here. The Fourteenth Amendment prohibits the police from using the private, secret custody of either man or child as a device for wringing confessions from them.

> *"In order to . . . permit a full opportunity to exercise the privilege against self-incrimination, the accused must be adequately and effectively apprised of his rights."*

Criminal Defendants Must Be Informed of Their Rights Prior to Interrogation

The Supreme Court's Decision

Earl Warren

In the following viewpoint, Earl Warren, writing for the majority of the US Supreme Court, contends that in order to protect the privilege against self-incrimination guaranteed by the Fifth Amendment, procedural safeguards must be adopted by law enforcement. Warren offers a framework for law enforcement for ensuring that interrogation is constitutional and, thus, information obtained is admissible into court proceedings. Outlining what has come to be known as the Miranda *warning, Warren says that suspects must be informed of their right to remain silent and their right to an attorney in order for their statements to be considered freely given and consistent with the guarantees of the Fifth Amendment. Warren served as chief justice of the Supreme Court from 1953 to 1969, an era of the court known for landmark decisions, among which is* Miranda v. Arizona *(1966).*

Earl Warren, *Miranda v. Arizona*, US Supreme Court, June 13, 1966.

The cases before us raise questions which go to the roots of our concepts of American criminal jurisprudence: the restraints society must observe consistent with the Federal Constitution in prosecuting individuals for crime. More specifically, we deal with the admissibility of statements obtained from an individual who is subjected to custodial police interrogation and the necessity for procedures which assure that the individual is accorded his privilege under the Fifth Amendment to the Constitution not to be compelled to incriminate himself. . . .

The Need for Limits on Custodial Interrogation

The constitutional issue we decide in each of these cases is the admissibility of statements obtained from a defendant questioned while in custody or otherwise deprived of his freedom of action in any significant way. In each, the defendant was questioned by police officers, detectives, or a prosecuting attorney in a room in which he was cut off from the outside world. In none of these cases was the defendant given a full and effective warning of his rights at the outset of the interrogation process. In all the cases, the questioning elicited oral admissions, and in three of them, signed statements as well which were admitted at their trials. They all thus share salient features—incommunicado interrogation of individuals in a police-dominated atmosphere, resulting in self-incriminating statements without full warnings of constitutional rights.

An understanding of the nature and setting of this in-custody interrogation is essential to our decisions today. The difficulty in depicting what transpires at such interrogations stems from the fact that, in this country, they have largely taken place incommunicado. From extensive factual studies undertaken in the early 1930s, including the famous Wickersham Report to Congress by a Presidential Commission, it is clear that police violence and the "third degree" flourished at that time. In a series of cases decided by this Court long after these studies, the police resorted to physical brutality—beating, hanging, whipping—and to sustained and protracted questioning incommunicado in order to extort confessions. The Commission on Civil Rights in 1961 found much evidence to indicate that "some policemen still resort to physical force to obtain confessions." The use of physical brutality and violence is not, unfortunately, relegated to the past or to any part of the country. Only recently in Kings County, New York, the police brutally beat, kicked and placed lighted cigarette butts on the back of a potential witness under interrogation for the purpose of securing a statement incriminating a third party.

The examples given above are undoubtedly the exception now, but they are sufficiently widespread to be the object of concern. Unless a proper limitation upon custodial interrogation is achieved—such as these decisions will advance—there can be no assurance that practices of this nature will be eradicated in the foreseeable future. . . .

The Practice of Incommunicado Interrogation

In the cases before us today, given this background, we concern ourselves primarily with this interrogation atmosphere and the evils it can bring. In No. 759, *Miranda v. Arizona*, the police arrested the defendant and took him to a special interrogation room, where they secured a confession. In No. 760, *Vignera v. New York*, the defendant made oral admissions to the police after interrogation in the afternoon, and then signed an inculpatory statement upon being questioned by an assistant district attorney later the same evening. In No. 761, *Westover v. United States*, the defendant was handed over to the Federal Bureau of Investigation by local authorities after they had detained and interrogated him for a lengthy period, both at night and the following morning. After some two hours of questioning, the federal officers had obtained signed statements from the defendant. Lastly, in No. 584, *California v. Stewart*, the local police held the defendant five days

Carroll Cooley (left) was the arresting officer in Miranda v. Arizona *(1966), the landmark case that requires law enforcement officials to inform criminal suspects of their rights upon arrest.* © Matt York/AP Images.

in the station and interrogated him on nine separate occasions before they secured his inculpatory statement.

In these cases, we might not find the defendants' statements to have been involuntary in traditional terms. Our concern for adequate safeguards to protect precious Fifth Amendment rights is, of course, not lessened in the slightest. In each of the cases, the defendant was thrust into an unfamiliar atmosphere and run through menacing police interrogation procedures. The potentiality for compulsion is forcefully apparent, for example, in *Miranda*, where the indigent Mexican defendant was a seriously disturbed individual with pronounced sexual fantasies, and in *Stewart*, in which the defendant was an indigent Los Angeles Negro who had dropped out of school in the sixth grade. To be sure, the records do not evince overt physical coercion or patent psychological ploys. The fact remains that in none of these cases did the officers undertake to afford appropriate safeguards at the outset of the interrogation to ensure that the statements were truly the product of free choice.

It is obvious that such an interrogation environment is created for no purpose other than to subjugate the individual to the will of his examiner. This atmosphere carries its own badge of intimidation. To be sure, this is not physical intimidation, but it is equally destructive of human dignity. The current practice of incommunicado interrogation is at odds with one of our Nation's most cherished principles—that the individual may not be compelled to incriminate himself. Unless adequate protective devices are employed to dispel the compulsion inherent in custodial surroundings, no statement obtained from the defendant can truly be the product of his free choice.

From the foregoing, we can readily perceive an intimate connection between the privilege against self-incrimination and police custodial questioning. It is fitting to turn to history and precedent underlying the Self-incrimination Clause to determine its applicability in this situation.

The Historical Roots of the Privilege Against Self-Incrimination

We sometimes forget how long it has taken to establish the privilege against self-incrimination, the sources from which it came, and the fervor with which it was defended. Its roots go back into ancient times. Perhaps the critical historical event shedding light on its origins and evolution was the trial of one John Lilburn, a vocal anti-Stuart Leveller, who was made to take the Star Chamber Oath in 1637. The oath would have bound him to answer to all questions posed to him on any subject. He resisted the oath and declaimed the proceedings, stating:

> Another fundamental right I then contended for was that no
> man's conscience ought to be racked by oaths imposed to an-

swer to questions concerning himself in matters criminal, or pretended to be so. [William Haller and Godfrey Davies, *The Leveller Tracts 1647–1653*, (1944)].

On account of the Lilburn Trial, Parliament abolished the inquisitorial Court of Star Chamber and went further in giving him generous reparation. The lofty principles to which Lilburn had appealed during his trial gained popular acceptance in England. These sentiments worked their way over to the Colonies, and were implanted after great struggle into the Bill of Rights. Those who framed our Constitution and the Bill of Rights were ever aware of subtle encroachments on individual liberty. They knew that

> illegitimate and unconstitutional practices get their first footing . . . by silent approaches and slight deviations from legal modes of procedure. [*Boyd v. United States* (1886)].

The privilege was elevated to constitutional status, and has always been "as broad as the mischief against which it seeks to guard" [*Counselman v. Hitchcock* (1892)].We cannot depart from this noble heritage. . . .

The Need to Informed Accused Persons of Their Rights

Today, then, there can be no doubt that the Fifth Amendment privilege is available outside of criminal court proceedings, and serves to protect persons in all settings in which their freedom of action is curtailed in any significant way from being compelled to incriminate themselves. We have concluded that, without proper safeguards, the process of in-custody interrogation of persons suspected or accused of crime contains inherently compelling pressures which work to undermine the individual's will to resist and to compel him to speak where he would not otherwise do so freely. In order to combat these pressures and to permit a full opportunity to exercise the privilege against self-incrimination, the

UNDERSTANDING OF *MIRANDA* RIGHTS BY DEFENDANTS

Percentage of defendants who misunderstood the following statements:

The statement, "You have the right to remain silent," means that your silence cannot be used against you at trial.	30.9%
If you remain silent, your silence can and will be used as evidence against you.	31.1%
The longer you remain silent, the more charges the police will bring against you.	9.4%

Taken from: Richard Rogers, Jill E. Rogstad, Nathan D. Gillard, et al., "Everyone Knows Their Miranda Rights': Implicit Assumptions and Countervailing Evidence," *Psychology, Public Policy, and Law*, vol. 16, no. 3, 2010.

accused must be adequately and effectively apprised of his rights, and the exercise of those rights must be fully honored.

It is impossible for us to foresee the potential alternatives for protecting the privilege which might be devised by Congress or the States in the exercise of their creative rulemaking capacities. Therefore, we cannot say that the Constitution necessarily requires adherence to any particular solution for the inherent compulsions of the interrogation process as it is presently conducted. Our decision in no way creates a constitutional straitjacket which will handicap sound efforts at reform, nor is it intended to have this effect. We encourage Congress and the States to continue their laudable search for increasingly effective ways of protecting the rights of the individual while promoting efficient enforcement of our criminal laws. However, unless we are shown other procedures which are at least as effective in apprising accused persons of their right of silence and in assuring a continuous opportunity to exercise it, the following safeguards must be observed.

At the outset, if a person in custody is to be subjected to interrogation, he must first be informed in clear and unequivocal terms that he has the right to remain silent. For those unaware of the privilege, the warning is needed simply to make them aware of it—the threshold requirement for an intelligent decision as to its exercise. More important, such a warning is an absolute prerequisite in overcoming the inherent pressures of the interrogation atmosphere. It is not just the subnormal or woefully ignorant who succumb to an interrogator's imprecations, whether implied or expressly stated, that the interrogation will continue until a confession is obtained or that silence in the face of accusation is itself damning, and will bode ill when presented to a jury. Further, the warning will show the individual that his interrogators are prepared to recognize his privilege should he choose to exercise it.

The Development of *Miranda* Rights

The Fifth Amendment privilege is so fundamental to our system of constitutional rule, and the expedient of giving an adequate warning as to the availability of the privilege so simple, we will not pause to inquire in individual cases whether the defendant was aware of his rights without a warning being given. Assessments of the knowledge the defendant possessed, based on information as to his age, education, intelligence, or prior contact with authorities, can never be more than speculation; warning is a clear-cut fact. More important, whatever the background of the person interrogated, a warning at the time of the interrogation is indispensable to overcome its pressures and to insure that the individual knows he is free to exercise the privilege at that point in time.

The warning of the right to remain silent must be accompanied by the explanation that anything said can and will be used against the individual in court. This warning is needed in order to make him aware not only of the privilege, but also of the consequences of forgoing it. It is only through an awareness of these consequences that there can be any assurance of real understanding and intelligent exercise of the privilege. Moreover, this warning may serve to make the individual more acutely aware that he is faced with a phase of the adversary system—that he is not in the presence of persons acting solely in his interest.

The circumstances surrounding in-custody interrogation can operate very quickly to overbear the will of one merely made aware of his privilege by his interrogators. Therefore, the right to have counsel present at the interrogation is indispensable to the protection of the Fifth Amendment privilege under the system we delineate today. Our aim is to assure that the individual's right to choose between silence and speech remains unfettered throughout the interrogation process. A once-stated warning, delivered by those who will conduct the interrogation, cannot itself suffice to that end among those who most require knowledge of their rights. A mere warning given by the interrogators is not alone sufficient to accomplish that end. Prosecutors themselves claim that the admonishment of the right to remain silent, without more, "will benefit only the recidivist and the professional." Even preliminary advice given to the accused by his own attorney can be swiftly overcome by the secret interrogation process. Thus, the need for counsel to protect the Fifth Amendment privilege comprehends not merely a right to consult with counsel prior to questioning, but also to have counsel present during any questioning if the defendant so desires. . . .

Once warnings have been given, the subsequent procedure is clear. If the individual indicates in any manner, at any time prior to or during questioning, that he wishes to remain silent, the interrogation must cease. At this point, he has shown that he intends to exercise his Fifth Amendment privilege; any statement taken after the person invokes his privilege cannot be other than the product of compulsion, subtle or otherwise. Without the right to cut off questioning, the setting of in-custody interrogation operates on the individual to overcome free choice in producing a statement after the privilege has been once invoked. If the individual states that he wants an attorney, the interrogation must cease until an attorney is present. At that time, the individual must have an opportunity to confer with the attorney and to have him present during any subsequent questioning. If the individual cannot obtain an attorney and he indicates that he wants one before speaking to police, they must respect his decision to remain silent. . . .

Protecting the Privilege Against Self-Incrimination

The principles announced today deal with the protection which must be given to the privilege against self-incrimination when the individual is first subjected to police interrogation while in custody at the station or otherwise deprived of his freedom of action in any significant way. It is at this point that our adversary system of criminal proceedings commences, distinguishing itself at the outset from the inquisitorial system recognized in some countries. Under the system of warnings we delineate today, or under any other system which may be devised and found effective, the safeguards to be erected about the privilege must come into play at this point.

Our decision is not intended to hamper the traditional function of police officers in investigating crime. When an individual is in custody on probable cause, the police may, of course, seek out evidence in the field to be used at trial against him. Such investigation may include inquiry of persons not under restraint. General on-the-scene questioning as to facts surrounding a crime or other general questioning of citizens in the factfinding process is not affected by our holding. It is an act of responsible citizenship for individuals to give whatever information they may have to aid in law enforcement. In such situations, the compelling atmosphere inherent in the process of in-custody interrogation is not necessarily present.

In dealing with statements obtained through interrogation, we do not purport to find all confessions inadmissible. Confessions remain a proper element in law enforcement. Any statement given freely and voluntarily without any compelling influences is, of course, admissible in evidence. The fundamental import of the privilege while an individual is in custody is not whether he is allowed to talk to the police without the benefit of warnings and counsel, but whether he can be interrogated. There is no requirement that police stop a person who enters a police station and states that he wishes to confess to a crime, or a person who calls the police to offer a confession or any other statement he desires to make. Volunteered statements of any kind are not barred by the Fifth Amendment, and their admissibility is not affected by our holding today.

To summarize, we hold that, when an individual is taken into custody or otherwise deprived of his freedom by the authorities in any significant way and is subjected to questioning, the privilege against self-incrimination is jeopardized. Procedural safeguards must be employed to protect the privilege, and unless other fully effective means are adopted to notify the person of his right of silence and to assure that the exercise of the right will be scrupulously honored, the following measures are required. He must be warned prior to any questioning that he has the right to remain silent, that anything he says can be used against him in a court of law, that he has the right to the presence of an attorney, and that, if he cannot afford an attorney one will be appointed for him prior to any questioning if he so desires. Opportunity to exercise these rights must be afforded to him throughout the interrogation. After such warnings have been given, and such opportunity afforded him, the individual may knowingly and intelligently waive these rights and agree to answer questions or make a statement. But unless and until such warnings and waiver are demonstrated by the prosecution at trial, no evidence obtained as a result of interrogation can be used against him.

> *"The constitutional privilege against self-incrimination is applicable in the case of juveniles as it is with respect to adults."*

Juveniles Have the Same Rights as Adults When Accused of a Crime

The Supreme Court's Decision

Abe Fortas

In the following viewpoint, Abe Fortas, writing for the majority of the US Supreme Court, argues that juveniles who are accused of crimes in delinquency proceedings have the same due process rights as adults. Fortas concludes that juveniles have the same privilege against self-incrimination as adults and denies that there are valid reasons for denying juveniles their right to remain silent. He concludes that the juvenile proceeding that committed Gerald Gault to an institutional school denied him his constitutional rights. Fortas served as associate justice of the Supreme Court from 1965 to 1969.

On Monday, June 8, 1964, at about 10 A.M., Gerald Francis Gault and a friend, Ronald Lewis, were taken into custody

Abe Fortas, Majority Opinion, *In re Gault*, US Supreme Court, May 15, 1967.

by the Sheriff of Gila County. Gerald was then still subject to a six months' probation order which had been entered on February 25, 1964, as a result of his having been in the company of another boy who had stolen a wallet from a lady's purse. The police action on June 8 was taken as the result of a verbal complaint by a neighbor of the boys, Mrs. [Ora] Cook, about a telephone call made to her in which the caller or callers made lewd or indecent remarks. It will suffice for purposes of this opinion to say that the remarks or questions put to her were of the irritatingly offensive, adolescent, sex variety.

Gault Is Committed to a Juvenile Institution

At the time Gerald was picked up, his mother and father were both at work. No notice that Gerald was being taken into custody was left at the home. No other steps were taken to advise them that their son had, in effect, been arrested. Gerald was taken to the Children's Detention Home. . . .

On June 9, Gerald, his mother, his older brother, and Probation Officers Flagg and Henderson appeared before the Juvenile Judge in chambers. Gerald's father was not there. He was at work out of the city. Mrs. Cook, the complainant, was not there. No one was sworn at this hearing. No transcript or recording was made. No memorandum or record of the substance of the proceedings was prepared. Our information about the proceedings and the subsequent hearing on June 15, derives entirely from the testimony of the Juvenile Court Judge, Mr. and Mrs. Gault and Officer Flagg at the *habeas corpus* proceeding conducted two months later. From this, it appears that, at the June 9 hearing, Gerald was questioned by the judge about the telephone call. There was conflict as to what he said. His mother recalled that Gerald said he only dialed Mrs. Cook's number and handed the telephone to his friend, Ronald. Officer Flagg recalled that Gerald had admitted making the lewd remarks. Judge McGhee testified that Gerald "admitted making one of these [lewd] statements." At the conclusion of the hearing, the judge said he would "think about it." Gerald was taken back to the Detention Home. . . .

At this June 15 hearing a "referral report" made by the probation officers was filed with the court, although not disclosed to Gerald or his parents. This listed the charge as "Lewd Phone Calls." At the conclusion of the hearing, the judge committed Gerald as a juvenile delinquent to the State Industrial School "for the period of his minority [that is, until 21], unless sooner discharged by due process of law.". . .

The Juvenile Court Process

From the inception of the juvenile court system, wide differences have been tolerated—indeed insisted upon—between the procedural rights accorded to adults and those of juveniles. In practically all jurisdictions, there are rights granted to adults which are withheld from juveniles. In addition to the specific problems involved in the present case, for example, it has been held that the juvenile is not entitled to bail, to indictment by grand jury, to a public trial or to trial by jury. It is frequent practice that rules governing the arrest and interrogation of adults by the police are not observed in the case of juveniles. . . .

We confront the reality of that portion of the Juvenile Court process with which we deal in this case. A boy is charged with misconduct. The boy is committed to an institution where he may be restrained of liberty for years. It is of no constitutional consequence—and of limited practical meaning—that the institution to which he is committed is called an Industrial School. The fact of the matter is that, however euphemistic the title, a "receiving home" or an "industrial school" for juveniles is an institution of confinement in which the child is incarcerated for a greater or lesser time. His world becomes "a building with whitewashed walls, regimented routine and institutional hours. . . ." Instead of mother and father and sisters and brothers and friends and classmates, his world is peopled by guards, custodians, state

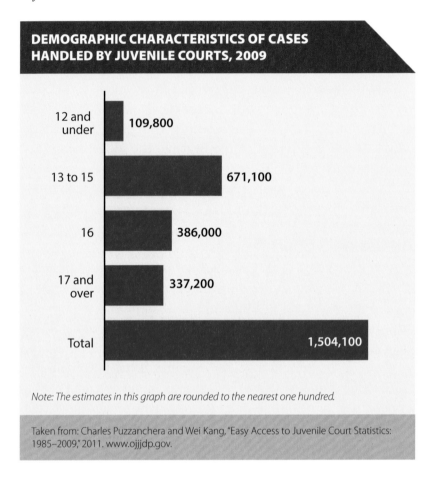

DEMOGRAPHIC CHARACTERISTICS OF CASES HANDLED BY JUVENILE COURTS, 2009

12 and under	109,800
13 to 15	671,100
16	386,000
17 and over	337,200
Total	1,504,100

Note: The estimates in this graph are rounded to the nearest one hundred.

Taken from: Charles Puzzanchera and Wei Kang, "Easy Access to Juvenile Court Statistics: 1985–2009," 2011. www.ojjdp.gov.

employees, and "delinquents" confined with him for anything from waywardness to rape and homicide.

In view of this, it would be extraordinary if our Constitution did not require the procedural regularity and the exercise of care implied in the phrase "due process." Under our Constitution, the condition of being a boy does not justify a kangaroo court. The traditional ideas of Juvenile Court procedure, indeed, contemplated that time would be available and care would be used to establish precisely what the juvenile did and why he did it—was it a prank of adolescence or a brutal act threatening serious consequences to himself or society unless corrected? Under traditional notions, one would assume that, in a case like that of Gerald Gault, where the juvenile appears to have a home, a working mother and father, and an older brother, the Juvenile Judge would have made a careful inquiry and judgment as to the possibility that the boy could be disciplined and dealt with at home, despite his previous transgressions. Indeed, so far as appears in the record before us, except for some conversation with Gerald about his school work and his "wanting to go to . . . Grand Canyon with his father," the points to which the judge directed his attention were little different from those that would be involved in determining any charge of violation of a penal statute. The essential difference between Gerald's case and a normal criminal case is that safeguards available to adults were discarded in Gerald's case. The summary procedure as well as the long commitment was possible because Gerald was 15 years of age instead of over 18.

If Gerald had been over 18, he would not have been subject to Juvenile Court proceedings. For the particular offense immediately involved, the maximum punishment would have been a fine of $5 to $50, or imprisonment in jail for not more than two months. Instead, he was committed to custody for a maximum of six years. If he had been over 18 and had committed an offense to which such a sentence might apply, he would have been entitled to substantial rights under the Constitution of the United States as well as under Arizona's laws and constitution. The United States Constitution would guarantee him rights and protections with respect to arrest, search and seizure, and pretrial interrogation. It would assure him of specific notice of the charges and adequate time to decide his course of action and to prepare his defense. He would be entitled to clear advice that he could be represented by counsel, and, at least if a felony were involved, the State would be required to provide counsel if his parents were unable to afford it. If the court acted on the basis of his confession, careful procedures would be required to assure its voluntariness. If the case went to trial, confrontation and opportunity for cross-examination would be guaranteed. So wide a gulf between the State's treatment of the adult and of the child requires a bridge sturdier than mere verbiage, and reasons more persuasive than cliché can provide. . . .

Minors' Privilege Against Self-Incrimination

Neither Gerald nor his parents were advised that he did not have to testify or make a statement, or that an incriminating statement might result in his commitment as a "delinquent."

The Arizona Supreme Court rejected appellants' contention that Gerald had a right to be advised that he need not incriminate himself. It said:

> We think the necessary flexibility for individualized treatment will be enhanced by a rule which does not require the judge to advise the infant of a privilege against self-incrimination.

In reviewing this conclusion of Arizona's Supreme Court, we emphasize again that we are here concerned only with a proceeding to determine whether a minor is a "delinquent" and which may result in commitment to a state institution. Specifically, the question is whether, in such a proceeding, an admission by the juvenile may be used against him in the absence of clear and unequivocal evidence that the admission was made with knowledge that he was not obliged to speak and would not be penalized for remaining silent. In light of *Miranda v. Arizona* (1966), we must also consider whether, if the privilege against self-incrimination is available, it can effectively be waived unless counsel is present or the right to counsel has been waived.

It has long been recognized that the eliciting and use of confessions or admissions require careful scrutiny. . . .

This Court has emphasized that admissions and confessions of juveniles require special caution. . . .

The privilege against self-incrimination is, of course, related to the question of the safeguards necessary to assure that admissions or confessions are reasonably trustworthy, that they are not the mere fruits of fear or coercion, but are reliable expressions of the truth. The roots of the privilege are, however, far deeper. They tap the basic stream of religious and political principle, because the privilege reflects the limits of the individual's attornment to the state and—in a philosophical sense—insists upon the equality of the individual and the state. In other words, the privilege has a broader and deeper thrust than the rule which prevents the use of confessions which are the product of coercion because coercion is thought to carry with it the danger of unreliability. One of its purposes is to prevent the state, whether by force or by psychological domination, from overcoming the mind and will of the person under investigation and depriving him of the freedom to decide whether to assist the state in securing his conviction.

It would indeed be surprising if the privilege against self-incrimination were available to hardened criminals, but not to children. The language of the Fifth Amendment, applicable to the States by operation of the Fourteenth Amendment, is unequivocal and without exception. And the scope of the privilege is comprehensive. . . .

The Arguments Against Juvenile Rights

Against the application to juveniles of the right to silence, it is argued that juvenile proceedings are "civil," and not "criminal," and therefore the privilege should not apply. It is true that the statement of the privilege in the Fifth Amendment, which is applicable to the States by reason of the Fourteenth Amendment, is that no person "shall be compelled in any criminal case to be a witness against himself." However, it is also clear that the availability of the privilege does not turn upon the type of proceeding in which its protection is invoked, but upon the nature of the statement or admission and the exposure which it invites. The privilege may, for example, be claimed in a civil or administrative proceeding, if the statement is or may be inculpatory.

It would be entirely unrealistic to carve out of the Fifth Amendment all statements by juveniles on the ground that these cannot lead to "criminal" involvement. In the first place, juvenile proceedings to determine "delinquency," which may lead to commitment to a state institution, must be regarded as "criminal" for purposes of the privilege against self-incrimination. To hold otherwise would be to disregard substance because of the feeble enticement of the "civil" "label of convenience" which has been attached to juvenile proceedings. Indeed, in over half of the States, there is not even assurance that the juvenile will be kept in separate institutions, apart from adult "criminals." In those States, juveniles may be placed in or transferred to adult penal institutions after having been found "delinquent" by a juvenile court. For this purpose, at least, commitment is a deprivation of liberty. It is incarceration against one's will, whether it is called "criminal" or "civil." And our Constitution guarantees that no person shall be "compelled" to be a witness against himself when he is threatened with deprivation of his liberty—a command which this Court has broadly applied and generously implemented in accordance with the teaching of the history of the privilege and its great office in mankind's battle for freedom.

In addition, apart from the equivalence for this purpose of exposure to commitment as a juvenile delinquent and exposure to imprisonment as an adult offender, the fact of the matter is that there is little or no assurance in Arizona, as in most if not all of the States, that a juvenile apprehended and interrogated by the police or even by the Juvenile Court itself will remain outside of the reach of adult courts as a consequence of the offense for which he has been taken into custody. In Arizona, as in other States, provision is made for Juvenile Courts to relinquish or waive jurisdiction to the ordinary criminal courts. In the present case, when Gerald Gault was interrogated concerning violation of a section of the Arizona Criminal Code, it could not be certain that the Juvenile Court Judge would decide to "suspend" crimi-

Gerald Gault (center) was the plaintiff in the US Supreme Court case In re Gault *(1967). The court ruled that juveniles have the same due process rights as adults, and the juvenile system that committed Gault to an institutional school violated his constitutional rights.* © Ernest K. Bennett/AP Images.

nal prosecution in court for adults by proceeding to an adjudication in Juvenile Court.

It is also urged, as the Supreme Court of Arizona here asserted, that the juvenile and presumably his parents should not be advised of the juvenile's right to silence because confession is good for the child as the commencement of the assumed therapy of the juvenile court process, and he should be encouraged to assume an attitude of trust and confidence toward the officials of the juvenile process. This proposition has been subjected to widespread challenge on the basis of current reappraisals of the rhetoric and realities of the handling of juvenile offenders.

In fact, evidence is accumulating that confessions by juveniles do not aid in "individualized treatment," as the court below put it, and that compelling the child to answer questions, without warning or advice as to his right to remain silent, does not serve this or any other good purpose. . . .

The Need to Respect Juveniles' Rights

We conclude that the constitutional privilege against self-incrimination is applicable in the case of juveniles as it is with respect to adults. We appreciate that special problems may arise with respect to waiver of the privilege by or on behalf of children, and that there may well be some differences in technique—but not in principle—depending upon the age of the child and the presence and competence of parents. The participation of counsel will, of course, assist the police, Juvenile Courts and appellate tribunals in administering the privilege. If counsel was not present for some permissible reason when an admission was obtained, the greatest care must be taken to assure that the admission was voluntary, in the sense not only that it was not coerced or suggested, but also that it was not the product of ignorance of rights or of adolescent fantasy, fright or despair.

The "confession" of Gerald Gault was first obtained by Officer Flagg, out of the presence of Gerald's parents, without counsel and without advising him of his right to silence, as far as appears. The judgment of the Juvenile Court was stated by the judge to be based on Gerald's admissions in court. Neither "admission" was reduced to writing, and, to say the least, the process by which the "admissions" were obtained and received must be characterized as lacking the certainty and order which are required of proceedings of such formidable consequences. Apart from the "admissions," there was nothing upon which a judgment or finding might be based. There was no sworn testimony. Mrs. Cook, the complainant, was not present. The Arizona Supreme Court held that

> sworn testimony must be required of all witnesses including police officers, probation officers and others who are part of or officially related to the juvenile court structure.

We hold that this is not enough. No reason is suggested or appears for a different rule in respect of sworn testimony in juvenile courts than in adult tribunals. Absent a valid confession adequate to support the determination of the Juvenile Court, confrontation and sworn testimony by witnesses available for cross-examination were essential for a finding of "delinquency" and an order committing Gerald to a state institution for a maximum of six years.

The recommendations in the Children's Bureau's "Standards for Juvenile and Family Courts" are in general accord with our conclusions. They state that testimony should be under oath and that only competent, material and relevant evidence under rules applicable to civil cases should be admitted in evidence. The New York Family Court Act contains a similar provision.

As we said in *Kent v. United States* (1966), with respect to waiver proceedings, "there is no place in our system of law for reaching a result of such tremendous consequences without ceremony. . . ." We now hold that, absent a valid confession, a determination of delinquency and an order of commitment to a state institution cannot be sustained in the absence of sworn testimony subjected to the opportunity for cross-examination in accordance with our law and constitutional requirements.

> "*Principally,* Miranda *has eroded the supply of information available to law enforcement by introducing the criminal's defense attorney to the process at the earliest possible stage.*"

The *Miranda* Decision Has Had an Adverse Effect on the Criminal Justice System

Paul Cassell and Stephen J. Markman

In the following viewpoint, Paul Cassell and Stephen J. Markman argue that the US Supreme Court's 1966 ruling establishing the requirement of Miranda *warnings has hampered the effectiveness of the criminal justice system. The authors claim that the impact of* Miranda v. Arizona *has eliminated confession evidence, thereby reducing the number of convictions of criminals. Cassell and Markman claim that the language of the Fifth Amendment did not require the* Miranda *decision, and they claim the rights created by* Miranda *are not the best way to protect the privilege against self-incrimination. Cassell holds the Ronald N. Boyce Presidential Endowed Chair in Criminal Law at the S.J. Quinney College of Law at the University of Utah and is a former district court judge. Markman is a justice of the Michigan Supreme Court.*

Paul Cassel and Stephan J. Markman, "Miranda's Hidden Costs," *National Review*, vol. 47, no. 24, December 25, 1995, pp. 30–33. Copyright © 1995 by National Review. All rights reserved. Reproduced by permission.

Curiously absent from the debate within Congress about how to combat historically unprecedented levels of violent crime in the United States has been any serious discussion of the single most damaging legacy of the Supreme Court's criminal-justice revolution of the 1960s: the *Miranda* rule. While intensive debate has focused upon other aspects of the Court's revolution—for example, the exclusionary rule and novel forms of *habeas-corpus* review—*Miranda* today seems little more than an anachronistic remnant of the era of "Impeach Earl Warren" billboards.

One possible explanation for this development is that the impact of *Miranda*, while extraordinarily detrimental to the criminal-justice system, is largely a hidden one, while the costs of such innovations as the exclusionary rule and habeas corpus are highly visible, in the form of kilos of cocaine being removed from the courtroom and repetitive criminal appeals inundating the justice system. Indeed, the costs of *Miranda* are so obscured that even many law-enforcement officers are only vaguely aware of them. Estimating the costs of *Miranda* requires that we engage in the difficult exercise of comparing the present reality with the reality which might exist "but for" the rule.

For tens of millions of Americans, the *Miranda* warnings have been learned from countless televised police dramas in which arrested suspects have been apprised by conscientious police officers that "You have the right to remain silent; what you say may be used against you; you have a right to an attorney; and you have a right to a free attorney if you cannot afford one." Few of those who have long since memorized these innocuous words have paused to consider how they have eroded the ability of the criminal-justice system to carry out its responsibilities.

In its 1966 decision in *Miranda v. Arizona*, the Supreme Court by a 5 to 4 vote determined that the Fifth Amendment's prohibition against a person's being "compelled in any criminal case to be a witness against himself" required what have become known as the *Miranda* warnings whenever a witness in custody is subject to questioning by the police. The decision also required that police obtain a "waiver of rights" from a suspect—that is, an affirmative agreement from the suspect that he would like to talk to police. Also, if at any time the suspect indicated a wish to stop talking or to see a lawyer, police had to stop questioning immediately. Failure to deliver the warnings, obtain the waiver, or cut off questioning when requested automatically bars the use at trial of statements obtained from the suspect.

Underlying *Miranda* was a deep suspicion on the part of the Court majority about any custodial interrogation of criminal suspects. For the 175 years preceding *Miranda*, it had never been thought that the police were violating a suspect's constitutional rights merely by questioning him in the absence of an attorney. No, we are not referring to a police officer's beating the hapless suspect with a rubber hose or policemen working in shifts to keep the suspect from sleep until he finally confesses to a crime. Such tactics were condemned uniformly well before *Miranda*. To satisfy the requirements of the Fifth Amendment, a confession needed to be voluntary, and circumstances which called that voluntariness into doubt served to undermine the admissibility of a confession. Confessions occur for any number of reasons, including the simple desire to cleanse one's soul and the more complicated desire to explain extenuating circumstances. Under the voluntariness standard, police were not precluded from asking the suspect what knowledge he possessed about the dead body they had discovered buried in his backyard.

This old understanding of the Fifth Amendment's prohibition against coerced self-incrimination was sharply transformed by *Miranda*. The Court acknowledged that "it might not find the defendant's statements to have been involuntary in traditional terms." In other words, the *Miranda* decision was amending the Constitution. In place of the previous understanding, the Court effectively provided a criminal suspect with a right not to be questioned. If he was questioned prior to the warnings, any statements would be suppressed; if he was questioned after the warnings and after he had requested an attorney, any statements that were made prior to the attorney's arrival again would be suppressed. After the attorney's arrival, it was certain that there would be no statements at all.

In dissent, Justice Byron White observed, "In some unknown number of cases the Court's rule will return a killer, a rapist, or other criminal to the streets and to the environment which produced him to repeat his crime whenever it pleases him. As a consequence there will not be a gain, but a loss, in human dignity." Justice White was prescient, although it can hardly be imagined that the majority of Justices in *Miranda* disagreed with his assessment. Such a result was logically certain under *Miranda*.

The insidiousness of *Miranda* is that, by and large, the violent predators placed back on the streets are *not* suspects to whom police have failed to give proper warnings. After nearly three decades, the police not surprisingly have learned *Miranda* by rote and only rarely fail to administer its warnings or follow its waiver and questioning-cutoff rules. Relatively few criminal cases involve the suppression of evidence obtained by police after a failure to comply with *Miranda*. This is what many observers, including some law-enforcement officers themselves, mean when they contend that the system has "learned to live" with *Miranda*.

No, the enormous cost of *Miranda* is entailed not in the lapses of the system but in its successes. It is when the warnings are properly administered and waiver rules are followed that it wreaks its greatest harm. For what it has done is to substantially dry up access to a hugely important category of criminal evidence—confession evidence. It is almost as if the Supreme Court had told law-enforcement officials that, henceforth, they were no longer going to be able to use fingerprint evidence. No one would doubt that in "some unknown number of cases" individuals who would otherwise have been correctly identified as criminals would avoid prosecution.

Principally, *Miranda* has eroded the supply of information available to law enforcement by introducing the criminal's defense attorney to the process at the earliest possible stage. This

New technologies such as self-mounted video cameras allow police officers to obtain complete audio and video records of their work. Some maintain that videotaping has improved police interrogation practices and provided more protection for criminal suspects. © Eduardo Barraza/Demotix/Corbis.

is done, in a sense, by the suspect asserting his *Miranda* right to have an attorney present at questioning even before formal charges have been filed. The effect of this is to preclude entirely the questioning of many suspects because police recognize that such questioning would be pointless. By effectively insulating the suspect who invokes his rights or asks for a lawyer from any questioning, no matter how restrained or reasonable, *Miranda* has assured that far fewer confessions will be induced by questioning. For the *Miranda* majority, this was cause for celebration, not concern. But this is an odd—not to say dangerous—view of the world. As an earlier Supreme Court said, "the Constitution is not at all offended when a guilty man stubs his toe. On the contrary, it is decent to hope that he will." The principal legacy of *Miranda* is the creation of an environment in which everything possible has been done to avoid such self-inflicted injuries. Given the relatively modest intellectual faculties of many violent criminals, the incidence of such injuries had always been significant.

If the criminal suspect incriminates himself through police methods that do not involve compulsion, that is a good thing. It is a good thing because it results in accurate fact-finding by the criminal-justice system; it avoids the possibility that an innocent person might be charged with a crime he did not commit; and it promotes public confidence that the police have caught the right person. In other words, it is a good thing because it promotes justice through procedures which most Americans would view as fair.

The most compelling evidence of the desirability of confessions, and of the extent to which Justice White's warnings have been borne out, comes from the before-and-after studies done in the immediate wake of the decision in 1966. One leading study, done in Philadelphia, reported that, before *Miranda*, an estimated 45 per cent of all criminal suspects made confessions to police officers; following *Miranda*, that figure dropped to approximately 20 per cent. Another study, done in New York City, found that confession rates fell from 49 per cent to 15 per cent. In Pittsburgh, the confession rate among suspected robbers and murderers fell from 60 per cent to 30 per cent. Adverse effects on confessions were also reported in Chicago, Kansas City, Brooklyn, and New Orleans. The best-estimate consensus among all the studies done on the impact of *Miranda* is that a lost confession occurs in approximately one of every six, or 16 per cent, of all criminal cases in the United States.

The other leading methodology for such calculations, albeit less exact, is to compare the American confession rate after *Miranda* with confession rates in countries that follow different approaches to regulating police interrogations. Such comparisons fully confirm the conclusions of the before-and-after studies. Since *Miranda*, American police appear to obtain confessions in perhaps 40 per cent of all cases. In other countries, police are far more successful. In Great Britain in the 1970s and early 1980s, police, following the "Judges' Rules," gave only a very limited advice of rights. Confession rates were estimated to be 61 to 85 per cent, well above reported American rates. In Canada, confession rates also appear to be substantially higher than in the post-*Miranda* United States.

Such declines in confession rates as have occurred in the United States since *Miranda* are extraordinarily harmful to the interests of effective law enforcement. Confession evidence, because it comes from the perpetrator himself, is compelling; but it doesn't stand alone—it is virtually always subject to corroboration by physical or other evidence. According to the available studies, in about one-quarter (24 per cent) of all criminal cases, confessions or other self-incriminating statements by a suspect are indispensable to a criminal conviction; in many more cases, perhaps an equal number, it can be surmised that they make some difference in terms of the severity of the offense for which a defendant is convicted.

A rough calculation, then, can be made as to the real-world cost of the *Miranda* rules. Multiplying the estimated 16-point reduction in the confession rate after *Miranda* by the estimated 24 per cent of cases in which a confession was necessary for conviction produces a figure of 4 per cent of all criminal cases that will be "lost" or never successfully prosecuted because of the rules. That figure may not sound very high, but the cost in absolute numbers of criminal cases is staggering. For FBI-index crimes, each year *Miranda* results in approximately 28,000 "lost" cases for violent crimes (murder, rape, aggravated assault, and robbery) and 79,000 "lost" cases for serious property crimes (burglary, larceny, and car theft). The bare numbers do not begin to convey the human costs in murders that go unpunished, rapists who remain at large, and treasured heirlooms that are never recovered.

Additionally, the leverage of prosecutors would be reduced in a roughly equal number of cases, resulting in plea bargains more favorable to the defendant and less favorable to the public. Compare these figures with the likely gains expected from other crime-control measures, such as midnight basketball leagues or even long-overdue *habeas corpus* reform. It seems improbable that any other single needed change in the criminal-justice system would yield anywhere near the number of successful prosecutions that would result from repealing *Miranda*.

Further, all these figures must be weighed in the light of other figures from the Bureau of Justice Statistics indicating that roughly two-thirds of all violent crime in the United States is committed by repeat offenders. *Miranda* does not merely defeat justice in the immediate case, but prematurely returns to the streets individuals in this high-risk category.

If such a cost in "lost" prosecutions were compelled by the clear language of the Constitution or by the dictates of sound public policy, then society might intelligently choose to suffer the tragic consequences. However, the strictures of *Miranda* are not required by the Constitution—as the Supreme Court recognized in *Miranda* itself—nor are they improvements over alternative methods of achieving fairness and due process in the context of custodial questioning. *Miranda* instead is a "prophylactic" rule (by its own terms) designed to establish protections against violations of the Fifth Amendment. As Chief Justice Warren remarked in his opinion for the court, "[T]he Constitution does not require any specific code of procedures for protecting the privilege against self-incrimination during custodial interrogation. Congress and the States are free to develop their own safeguards for the privilege, so long as they are fully as effective [as the *Miranda* rules]." In a later decision, the Court reiterated that the *Miranda* rights "were not themselves rights protected by the Constitution but were instead measures to ensure that the right against compulsory self-incrimination was protected."

Responding to this invitation, Congress in 1968 enacted new legislation concerning police interrogation, adopting the view that such legislation would be "fully as effective" in maintaining the guarantees of the Fifth Amendment. The new law restored the traditional "voluntariness" test and identified the *Miranda* warnings as mere factors to be considered by the courts in deciding whether or not a confession was genuinely voluntary.

Because of the hostility of the incumbent attorney general, Ramsey Clark, who believed that it was unconstitutional, the new congressional enactment quickly fell into desuetude. United States Attorneys were ordered not to defend confessions unless they satisfied the *Miranda* standards. Although later attorneys general, including John Mitchell and Ed Meese, were cognizant of the statute and sensitive to the costs of *Miranda,* no serious efforts were undertaken to reverse the Johnson Administration policy or to secure any determination of the constitutionality of the law. A recommendation by the Justice Department's Office of Legal Policy in 1987 that an aggressive effort be made to test the law was never adopted as the result of opposition by other agencies within the Department.

The time has never been better for a test case raising the 1968 law and challenging *Miranda.* Just last year [1994], Justice [Antonin] Scalia wrote a scathing concurrence chastising the Justice Department for its failure to enforce the law. He observed that that failure "may have produced—during an era of intense national concern about the problem of run-away crime—the acquittal and non-prosecution of many dangerous felons, enabling them to continue their depredations upon our citizens." He promised to rule on the statute at the next available opportunity. Congress should make certain that the Justice Department gives him the opportunity by directing it to begin enforcing the statute and reminding the Executive Branch of its constitutional duty to "take care that the laws be faithfully executed." Congress need not enact a new law; it need only ensure that a law already on the books is presented to the Court.

A favorable Court ruling seems quite a realistic prospect. It has long been understood that the Congress has the final say on rules of evidence for federal cases. If the statute admitting voluntary confessions does not confront any constitutional barrier (as the Court has now plainly held), on what possible grounds could the enactment of the people's representatives be struck down? As the Office of Legal Policy observed in recommending that

"HOW DO YOU EXPECT ME TO CONCENTRATE WHEN YOU'RE READING ME MY RIGHTS?"

© Norman Jung/CartoonStock.com.

the legitimacy of the *Miranda*-repeal statute be asserted, "There is every reason to believe that an effort to correct this situation would be successful. . . . It is difficult to see how we could fail to make our case."

While the statute highlights the problems of *Miranda*'s continuing vitality in federal cases, equally perplexing is its applicability to the far greater number of state criminal prosecutions. The Supreme Court's acknowledgment that the *Miranda* rules are not derived from the Fifth Amendment leads one to ask how the federal judiciary possesses the authority to impose *Miranda* upon the states. It is an extraordinarily novel proposition of constitutional law that the states are limited in their criminal procedures not merely by the dictates of the Constitution but also by superintending or "prophylactic" rules invented by the federal judiciary. That such a proposition has not yet been challenged can be explained only by the states' tendency to rely upon the Justice Department for leadership on constitutional matters of this sort, as well, perhaps, as by an understandable failure even by the law-enforcement community to recognize the full extent of *Miranda*'s hidden costs.

Ironically, there are better means of enforcing the very protections toward which *Miranda* is directed. However, as is the case generally with the exercise of uniform national policies, *Miranda* petrified efforts by the states, which were widespread in the 1960s, to experiment with their custodial interrogation procedures and search for alternatives that might better protect not only society's interest in apprehending criminals but also suspects' interests in preventing coercive questioning.

Perhaps the most effective replacement for *Miranda* would simply be to videotape or record police interrogations. About one-sixth of all police departments in the country already videotape at least some confessions, and a recent study by the National Institute of Justice concluded that, in addition to providing safeguards for the suspect, videotaping also resulted in the improvement of police interrogation practices, rendered confessions more convincing to judges and juries, and assisted prosecutors in negotiating more favorable plea bargains and guilty pleas. Videotaping would also provide more protection for innocent suspects caught up in the criminal-justice system.

For *Miranda* is not particularly well tailored to protecting a suspect's rights to be free from coercion. Justice [John Marshall] Harlan's point in his *Miranda* dissent has never been effectively answered: "The new rules are not designed to guard against police brutality or other unmistakably banned forms of coercion. Those who use third-degree tactics and deny them in court are equally able and destined to lie as skillfully about warnings and waivers." It is not clear why police using rubber hoses before *Miranda* would have thought it necessary to shelve them afterward. Furthermore, once a valid *Miranda* waiver is obtained, police are relatively free to proceed as they like.

No legacy of the Warren Court has been more devastating to the first civil right of individuals, the right to be protected from attack. Congressional conservatives may choose to place serious procedural reform off-limits. They may do this, in part, because of the burdens of leadership required in order to explain the relationship of procedure to the substantive ability of the justice system to protect society. They may do this because it is easier to deal with public-policy problems whose costs are more visible. However, if effective reform is to be undertaken, unsettling such settled areas of the law as *Miranda* will be required. Until that time, society can do little more than continue to count Justice White's "unknown number" of killers, rapists, and other criminals who go free because of the criminal-justice innovations of the Warren Court.

> "Miranda *announced a constitutional rule that Congress may not supersede legislatively."*

The Requirement for *Miranda* Warnings Cannot Be Overruled by Legislation

The Supreme Court's Decision

William Rehnquist

In the following viewpoint, William Rehnquist, writing for the majority of the US Supreme Court, argues that the court's holding in Miranda v. Arizona *(1966) may not be overruled by an act of Congress. Rehnquist claims that the court's holding in* Miranda— *that in order for a suspect's statements to be admissible as evidence the suspect must have been given four warnings—announced a constitutional rule. Furthermore, Rehnquist claims that although not without disadvantages, the* Miranda *rule is preferable to a totality-of-the-circumstances test that proposed legislation sought to use as an alternative. Rehnquist was associate justice of the Supreme Court from 1972 to 1986 and was then appointed by President Ronald Reagan to the position of chief justice, a position he held until 2005.*

William Rehnquist, Majority Opinion, *Dickerson v. United States*, US Supreme Court, June 26, 2000.

In *Miranda v. Arizona*, (1966), we held that certain warnings must be given before a suspect's statement made during custodial interrogation could be admitted in evidence. In the wake of that decision, Congress enacted 18 U.S.C. § 3501 [Title 18 of the United States Code, Section 3501], which in essence laid down a rule that the admissibility of such statements should turn only on whether or not they were voluntarily made. We hold that *Miranda*, being a constitutional decision of this Court, may not be in effect overruled by an Act of Congress, and we decline to overrule *Miranda* ourselves. We therefore hold that *Miranda* and its progeny in this Court govern the admissibility of statements made during custodial interrogation in both state and federal courts. . . .

The Admissibility of Confessions

Prior to *Miranda*, we evaluated the admissibility of a suspect's confession under a voluntariness test. The roots of this test developed in the common law, as the courts of England and then the United States recognized that coerced confessions are inherently untrustworthy. Over time, our cases recognized two constitutional bases for the requirement that a confession be voluntary to be admitted into evidence: the Fifth Amendment right against self-incrimination and the Due Process Clause of the Fourteenth Amendment. . . .

In *Miranda*, we noted that the advent of modern custodial police interrogation brought with it an increased concern about confessions obtained by coercion. Because custodial police interrogation, by its very nature, isolates and pressures the individual, we stated that "[e]ven without employing brutality, the 'third degree' or [other] specific stratagems . . . custodial interrogation exacts a heavy toll on individual liberty and trades on the weakness of individuals." We concluded that the coercion inherent in custodial interrogation blurs the line between voluntary and involuntary statements, and thus heightens the risk that an individual will not be "accorded his privilege under the Fifth Amendment . . . not to be compelled to incriminate himself."

Accordingly, we laid down "concrete constitutional guidelines for law enforcement agencies and courts to follow." Those guidelines established that the admissibility in evidence of any statement given during custodial interrogation of a suspect would depend on whether the police provided the suspect with four warnings. These warnings (which have come to be known colloquially as "*Miranda* rights") are: a suspect "has the right to remain silent, that anything he says can be used against him in a court of law, that he has the right to the presence of an attorney, and that if he cannot afford an attorney one will be appointed for him prior to any questioning if he so desires."

An Act Intended to Overrule *Miranda*

Two years after *Miranda* was decided, Congress enacted § 3501. That section provides, in relevant part:

(a) In any criminal prosecution brought by the United States or by the District of Columbia, a confession . . . shall be admissible in evidence if it is voluntarily given. Before such confession is received in evidence, the trial judge shall, out of the presence of the jury, determine any issue as to voluntariness. If the trial judge determines that the confession was voluntarily made it shall be admitted in evidence and the trial judge shall permit the jury to hear relevant evidence on the issue of voluntariness and shall instruct the jury to give such weight to the confession as the jury feels it deserves under all the circumstances.

(b) The trial judge in determining the issue of voluntariness shall take into consideration all the circumstances surrounding the giving of the confession, including (1) the time elapsing between arrest and arraignment of the defendant making the confession, if it was made after arrest and before arraignment, (2) whether such defendant knew the nature of the offense with which he was charged or of which he was suspected at the time of making the confession, (3) whether or not such defendant was advised or knew that he was not required to make

The Constitutional Status of *Miranda*

Although there was reason to think the Court might uphold the constitutionality of § 3501 when the Court finally addressed the issue in the year 2000 (because of the post-Warren Court's characterizations of and comments about *Miranda* in the three decades since the case was decided), it is difficult to see how § 3501 could have passed constitutional muster had the Court decided its fate in 1938 or 1969. Indeed. I venture to say that *at the time* the *Miranda* opinion was handed down almost everyone who read it (including the dissenting Justices) understood that it was a constitutional decision—an interpretation of the Fifth Amendment privilege against self-incrimination.

Yale Kamisar, "Foreword: From Miranda to
§ 3501 to Dickerson to . . . ," Michigan Law
Review, vol. 99, no. 5, March 2001.

any statement and that any such statement could be used against him, (4) whether or not such defendant had been advised prior to questioning of his right to the assistance of counsel; and (5) whether or not such defendant was without the assistance of counsel when questioned and when giving such confession.

The presence or absence of any of the above-mentioned factors to be taken into consideration by the judge need not be conclusive on the issue of voluntariness of the confession.

Given §3501's express designation of voluntariness as the touchstone of admissibility, its omission of any warning requirement, and the instruction for trial courts to consider a nonexclusive list of factors relevant to the circumstances of a confession, we agree with the Court of Appeals that Congress intended by its enactment to overrule *Miranda*. Because of the obvious conflict between our decision in *Miranda* and § 3501, we must address whether Congress has constitutional authority to thus supersede *Miranda*. If Congress has such authority, § 3501's totality-of-the-circumstances approach must prevail over *Miranda*'s requirement of warnings; if not, that section must yield to *Miranda*'s more specific requirements.

The law in this area is clear. This Court has supervisory authority over the federal courts, and we may use that authority to prescribe rules of evidence and procedure that are binding in those tribunals. . . . Congress retains the ultimate authority to modify or set aside any judicially created rules of evidence and procedure that are not required by the Constitution.

But Congress may not legislatively supersede our decisions interpreting and applying the Constitution. This case therefore turns on whether the *Miranda* Court announced a constitutional rule or merely exercised its supervisory authority to regulate evidence in the absence of congressional direction. . . .

A Constitutional Rule

The *Miranda* opinion itself begins by stating that the Court granted certiorari [a writ issued by a superior court for the re-examination of an action of a lower court] "to explore some facets of the problems . . . of applying the privilege against self-incrimination to in-custody interrogation, *and to give concrete constitutional guidelines for law enforcement agencies and courts to follow*" (emphasis added). In fact, the majority opinion is replete with statements indicating that the majority thought it was announcing a constitutional rule. Indeed, the Court's ultimate conclusion was that the unwarned confessions obtained in the four cases before the Court in *Miranda*, "were obtained from the defendant under circumstances that did not meet constitutional standards for protection of the privilege."

Additional support for our conclusion that *Miranda* is constitutionally based is found in the *Miranda* Court's invitation for legislative action to protect the constitutional right against coerced self-incrimination. After discussing the "compelling pressures" inherent in custodial police interrogation, the *Miranda* Court concluded that, "[i]n order to combat these pressures and to permit a full opportunity to exercise the privilege against self-incrimination, the accused must be adequately and effectively apprised of his rights and the exercise of those rights must be fully honored." However, the Court emphasized that it could not foresee "the potential alternatives for protecting the privilege which might be devised by Congress or the States," and it accordingly opined that the Constitution would not preclude legislative solutions that differed from the prescribed *Miranda* warnings but which were "at least as effective in apprising accused persons of their right of silence and in assuring a continuous opportunity to exercise it.". . .

The dissent argues that it is judicial overreaching for this Court to hold § 3501 unconstitutional unless we hold that the *Miranda* warnings are required by the Constitution, in the sense that nothing else will suffice to satisfy constitutional requirements. But we need not go further than *Miranda* to decide this case. In *Miranda*, the Court noted that reliance on the traditional totality-of-the-circumstances test raised a risk of overlooking an involuntary custodial confession, a risk that the Court found unacceptably great when the confession is offered in the case in chief to prove guilt. The Court therefore concluded that something more than the totality test was necessary. As discussed above, § 3501 reinstates the totality test as sufficient. Section 3501 therefore cannot be sustained if *Miranda* is to remain the law.

The *Miranda* Rule Is Embedded in US Culture

We do not think there is such justification for overruling *Miranda*. *Miranda* has become embedded in routine police practice to the point where the warnings have become part of our national culture. While we have overruled our precedents when subsequent

The US Supreme Court has ruled that potential suspects have a constitutional right to be given the Miranda *warning upon arrest. In* Dickerson v. United States *(2000), the court upheld the* Miranda *rule and argued that it cannot be overturned by an act of Congress.* © Spencer Grant/ Photo Researchers/Getty Images.

cases have undermined their doctrinal underpinnings, we do not believe that this has happened to the *Miranda* decision. If anything, our subsequent cases have reduced the impact of the *Miranda* rule on legitimate law enforcement while reaffirming the decision's core ruling that unwarned statements may not be used as evidence in the prosecution's case in chief.

The disadvantage of the *Miranda* rule is that statements which may be by no means involuntary, made by a defendant who is aware of his "rights," may nonetheless be excluded and a guilty defendant go free as a result. But experience suggests that the totality-of-the-circumstances test which § 3501 seeks to revive is more difficult than *Miranda* for law enforcement officers to conform to, and for courts to apply in a consistent manner. The requirement that *Miranda* warnings be given does not, of course, dispense with the voluntariness inquiry. But as we said in *Berkemer v. McCarty* (1984), "[c]ases in which a defendant

can make a colorable argument that a self-incriminating statement was 'compelled' despite the fact that the law enforcement
authorities adhered to the dictates of *Miranda* are rare."

In sum, we conclude that *Miranda* announced a constitutional rule that Congress may not supersede legislatively.

> "The purpose of the Miranda *rule is to*
> *prevent forced confessions or, to put it*
> *more bluntly, torture."*

The Court Was Correct to Uphold the *Miranda* Rule

John P. Frank

In the following viewpoint, John P. Frank argues that the US Supreme Court's decision in Dickerson v. United States *(2000) will permanently fix the* Miranda *rule as settled law. Frank contends that the purpose of the* Miranda *rule is to prevent torture, and he argues that the rule has done good and not done harm. Frank claims that the Dickerson decision establishes that every person is entitled to know what is in the US Constitution. Frank was a lawyer and law professor who represented Ernesto Miranda in the landmark* Miranda v. Arizona *(1966) case, which established what has come to be known as the* Miranda *rule, requiring law enforcement to inform suspects of their rights under the Fifth Amendment.*

*M*iranda lives. Well, not the person. He died in a tavern brawl many years ago. The *Miranda* rule—the requirement that defendants must be told that "you have the right to re-

John P. Frank, "Miranda Ruling Shows Original's Sense," *Arizona Republic,* July 13, 2000, p. 5. Copyright © 2000 by Estate of John P. Frank. All rights reserved. Reproduced by permission.

main silent and to request counsel"—was reaffirmed by the U.S. Supreme Court on June 26 [2000].

The Background of the *Miranda* Requirement

Precisely what are we talking about? The Fifth Amendment to the U.S. Constitution provides that no person can testify against himself. This safeguard is meaningless if, before he gets to court, a witness has made damaging statements. By the time he gets to court, the constitutional protection will do him no good.

The *Miranda* case, which went to the Supreme Court from Arizona, established the rule that any person in custody must be told of his constitutional rights, and that if he was not, no statement he makes can be used against him ever.

This requirement came directly from the practice of the FBI. That agency, the prime police force in the country, had a fixed practice of telling people of their constitutional rights. What the Supreme Court did in *Miranda* [*v. Arizona* (1966)] was to require the countless state, city and county police officials throughout the country to do the same thing.

The Purpose of the *Miranda* Rule

The purpose of the *Miranda* rule is to prevent forced confessions or, to put it more bluntly, torture. It may be easier to get people to talk by beating them with a strap or rubbing pepper in their eyes. This has been done not only in communist or fascist countries, but in America as well. When Justice Hugo Black, one of the justices in the *Miranda* case, was a young prosecuting attorney in Alabama, he noticed that he was getting an astonishing large number of confessions from African-American defendants in Bessemer, Ala. This is because the defendants there, when they were brought to the police station, were strapped to a door and beaten until they confessed; and one of the problems is that people under torture may confess to stop the torture, whether they did it or not.

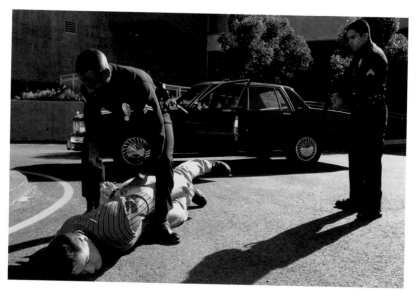

Some argue that the Miranda *rule, which requires law enforcement to inform suspects of their rights under the Fifth Amendment, benefits the criminal justice system.* © Kim Kulish/Corbis.

Chief Justice Earl Warren wrote the *Miranda* decision, and as attorney general and governor of California, he had seen the same kinds of abuse.

Immediately after *Miranda* was decided, there was considerable concern that guilty people might escape justice. Congress passed a statute restricting the *Miranda* rights. That statute had been ignored until last year [1999], when a federal court dug it up and applied it. It is that statute which was before the Supreme Court in the decision this year [2000].

In the intervening 34 years, the *Miranda* rule has proved to be sound police tactics. It has done good, and it has not done the harm that some people feared when it was decided.

The Court's Decision in *Dickerson v. United States*

A question of whether that act of Congress, restricting *Miranda* rights, was itself constitutional, finally reached the Supreme Court this year [2000]. On June 26, the Supreme Court ruled,

7-to-2, in an opinion by Chief Justice William Rehnquist, reaffirmed the *Miranda* rules and held unconstitutional an act of Congress that attempted to water them down.

"Coerced confessions are inherently untrustworthy," Rehnquist wrote in recognizing the problem: In reviewing earlier decisions, he said that they had held that "even without employing brutality or the third-degree," questioning a person who is in custody "exacts a heavy toll on individual liberty and trades on the weakness of individuals." *Miranda*, he said, requires that you at least give a suspect "four warnings" known as the "*Miranda* rights."

The main point of the chief justice was that in the 34-year period since *Miranda*, law enforcement systems of the country have adjusted to it. Its warnings, he said, have "become part of our national culture."

As a result, he said, it is now clearly established that "unwarned statements may not be used as evidence in the prosecution's case."

This 7-to-2 opinion is so decisive that it should establish for the future that every person in America, rich or poor, educated or uneducated, is governed by the Constitution. Every person in the United States, rich or poor, educated or uneducated, is entitled to know what is in the Constitution. *Miranda* says no more than this, but, as much as the Supreme Court of the United States can make it so, this will ever be our law.

| "While the Supreme Court is clearly
| unwilling to pull the plug, Miranda
| lingers at best on life support."

The Court's Upholding of Miranda in Dickerson Has Little Substance

Jonathan Turley

In the following viewpoint, Jonathan Turley argues that the US Supreme Court's decision in Dickerson v. United States *(2000) may have officially reaffirmed the* Miranda *rule, but there is little substance left to the protection of suspects' rights. Turley claims that because the court has created a myriad of exceptions to the* Miranda *rule, the impact of the ruling in* Miranda v. Arizona *(1966) has been watered down. Turley concludes that the court's decision upheld the mystique of the* Miranda *rule without truly requiring that criminal defendants be informed of their rights. Turley is the J.B. and Maurice C. Shapiro Professor of Public Interest Law at George Washington University Law School.*

"You have the right to remain silent. . . ." It's difficult to imagine what moviemakers would do without the required

Jonathan Turley, "Miranda—Confirmed, But Barely Alive," *Washington Post,* June 27, 2000, p. A23. Copyright © 2000 by Jon Turley. All rights reserved. Reproduced by permission.

Some argue that the Miranda rule does little to protect the rights of criminal suspects. The vast majority of suspects, between 80 and 90 percent, waive their Miranda *rights.* © Joe Raedle/ Getty Images.

Miranda warning to top off the arrest scene in just about every cop film they produce. So yesterday's [June 26, 2000] 7 to 2 vote by the Supreme Court upholding *Miranda* as a constitutional principle should be a comfort to Hollywood. For criminal defendants, however, *Miranda* will continue to make better dramas than defenses despite yesterday's ruling.

The Supreme Court Upholds
Dickerson v. United States

The survival of *Miranda* certainly came as a surprise to many who doubted both the decision's original basis in the Constitution and its remaining support on a more conservative court than the one that handed down the ruling in 1966, when even Chief Justice Earl Warren could eke out only a 5 to 4 majority from a liberal court.

Yet, Warren's most famous ruling was ultimately to be preserved by one of his most ardent critics, Chief Justice William

The Failure of *Miranda*

Miranda has not proved a major hindrance to police interrogators. Between 80 and 90 percent of all suspects waive their *Miranda* rights, and more than 90 percent of all felony convictions in America result from guilty pleas, either by confession or plea bargain. In short, *Miranda* has failed to achieve its original goal—allowing suspects to protect themselves against coercive police interrogation by cutting off questioning after it has started.

Jeffrey Rosen, *"Right Should Remain Silent: Don't End 'Miranda.' Mend It,"* New Republic, May 1, 2000.

Rehnquist. Putting to rest years of speculation over the viability and basis of the ruling, Rehnquist finally established that "*Miranda* is a constitutional decision" and, by extension, so are the progeny of cases that it inspired. As such, it is a rule that "Congress may not supersede legislatively."

But despite the sweeping language of yesterday's decision, there may be less to it than meets the eye. For while the Supreme Court is clearly unwilling to pull the plug, *Miranda* lingers at best on life support. In fact, the *Miranda* of the Warren Court died years ago. It succumbed not to a single blow of the conservative majority but to a thousand paper-cuts.

The Growing Exceptions to *Miranda*

Over the years, the Court has allowed a myriad of exceptions that make *Miranda* a mere symbolic presence in most federal cases. Because of these rulings, reversals of convictions under *Miranda* are relatively rare events.

For example, the Court ruled in 1984 that *Miranda* warnings are not necessary when the police seek information "reasonably prompted by a concern for the public safety." Under this "public safety exception," the police can question a suspect about the location of a gun and then use the evidence against him in court.

Likewise, the Court has limited the meaning of "custodial questioning" that triggers the *Miranda* protection. In a 1977 burglary case, the Court found that *Miranda* did not apply when the chief suspect was "invited" to come to the police station to discuss the crime.

Once a person is in "custody," the Court has narrowed the definition of "interrogation" by holding that "voluntary statements" are not protected, even when made in response to statements by the police. Thus, in a 1980 case a suspect was arrested for murder, and the officers engaged in an anguished discussion of the possibility that children from a nearby school for the handicapped might find the shotgun used in the crime. The suspect promptly incriminated himself by telling them where the gun was. The Court held that the officers could not have reasonably believed they would get such a response from the suspect.

Even after "interrogation" begins, the Court has allowed for police to secure waivers through acts of deception. For example, the Court upheld a waiver of *Miranda* rights in a 1986 murder case despite the fact that the police lied to a lawyer seeking access to the accused. After telling the lawyer that his client would not be interrogated, the police interrogated the suspect and secured a confession without ever disclosing that his family had hired a lawyer who was trying to see him.

The *Dickerson* Ruling Has Little Substance

Finally, even when the Court recognizes a clear violation of *Miranda*, it has allowed police to use the evidence. For example, in one of many cases limiting the "exclusionary rule," the Court ruled in a 1971 case that such evidence could be used to "impeach" a defendant if he takes the stand in his own defense.

Ultimately, what saved *Miranda* from being overturned is probably more its mystique than its meaning. *Miranda* has become too interwoven in our legal and cultural fabric to simply be dispatched as no longer relevant. The Court therefore preserved the body while allowing its spirit to drain away years ago.

There is a legitimate question as to whether *Miranda* is part of the Constitution, which does not expressly require a duty to inform defendants of their rights. But if it does indeed uphold a constitutional principle, there should be some substance to the protection. Otherwise, yesterday's reaffirmation of *Miranda* as constitutional law is little more than a constitutional affectation.

> *"Current case law ignores the
> Constitution's words, distorts
> constitutional structure and
> overprotects the guilty."*

Taking the Fifth Too Often

Akhil Reed Amar

In the following viewpoint, Akhil Reed Amar argues that the current legal understanding of the Fifth Amendment is a distortion of the US Constitution. Amar claims that a reading of the privilege against self-incrimination that allows individuals to refuse to testify before Congress has warped the separation of powers between the legislative and judicial branches of government, both by banning evidence that is obtained through testimony and by congressional avoidance of investigations that could lead to criminal findings. He proposes a rule allowing compelled testimony but preventing that testimony itself from being brought to criminal court. Amar is Sterling Professor of Law and Political Science at Yale University and author of America's Unwritten Constitution: The Precedents and Principles We Live By.

By what right do Enron bigwigs [corporation whose executives were found guilty of accounting fraud in 2001] stonewall

Akhil Reed Amar, "Taking the Fifth Too Often," *New York Times*, June 27, 2000, p. A1. Copyright © 2000 The New York Times. All rights reserved. Used by permission and protected by the Copyright Laws of the United States. The printing, copying, redistribution, or retransmission of this content without express written permission is prohibited.

Congress? The Fifth Amendment prohibits a person from being compelled to be a witness against himself in any "criminal case," but a Congressional hearing is hardly a criminal case.

The Need to Compel Testimony

The Fifth Amendment gives criminal defendants the right to refuse to testify at trial. Perhaps the most reasonable justification for this right is the need to protect innocent and truthful defendants from being made to appear guilty if forced to take the stand. They might well sweat, stutter or misspeak when pressured by crafty prosecutors, and be wrongly convicted.

To protect the core Fifth Amendment right, a person should also be allowed to "take the Fifth" outside his trial. Otherwise, prosecutors might simply be able to adjourn a trial, force the defendant to testify in some other setting, and then offer the transcript and videotape to the criminal jury.

But sometimes a truth-seeking society needs to be able to compel a person to speak outside his trial—grand jury rooms, civil cases and legislative hearings, for example. One solution is to require the person to testify in these specific places, but then exclude this compelled testimony from any later prosecution brought against him. This way, he would never become a witness against himself "in a criminal case."

This rule would offer Congressional witnesses a narrow type of testimonial immunity. While the testimony itself would be excluded from the criminal trial, evidence that might be drawn indirectly from the testimony would be admissible at a later trial. This would allow prosecutors to use any reliable leads that the testimony might generate. Courts today allow government lawyers to force people to give voice samples and take breath tests for alcohol because these are not considered forms of self-incrimination prohibited by the Fifth Amendment. If prosecutors can compel defendants to provide these kinds of evidence, they should also be allowed to introduce reliable evidence that is found as a result of earlier immunized testimony.

Oliver North received immunity for his testimony during the Iran-Contra congressional hearings in 1987. The Fifth Amendment is often invoked to avoid congressional testimony, and immunity is regularly given to compel witnesses to testify. © Chris Wilkins/AFP/Getty Images.

The US Supreme Court Puts a Ban on Evidence

This is exactly the rule that Congress enacted, and President Abraham Lincoln signed into law, in 1862. Two federal government clerks had embezzled bonds worth $2 million and then confessed in a Congressional hearing. They went on to claim that they could never be prosecuted because Congress had required them to talk. Congress cured the problem with a statute obliging future Congressional witnesses to speak when so ordered. Anyone refusing to speak could be held in contempt, and anyone lying could be charged with perjury—but all witnesses would be granted only narrow immunity, allowing later prosecutions based on leads generated in Congress. As one senator said at the time, restricted immunity was "all that a rascal ought to have at the hands of justice." If Congressional testimony led investigators to find other reliable bits of evidence to convict, so much the better.

But in 1892, the Supreme Court declared this statute unconstitutional. A person obliged to testify before Congress could never be prosecuted for anything related to his testimony, the court ruled. In later cases, the court softened this rule—a person forced to testify before Congress could be prosecuted so long as the testimony and all evidence found as a result of that testimony were excluded.

The Supreme Court has never explained where this ban on other evidence is to be found in the Fifth Amendment's words. Nor has the court explained how such a ban fits the general innocence-protecting idea that justifies the Fifth Amendment in the first place.

A Distortion of the Constitution

This longstanding reading of the Fifth Amendment has warped the separation of powers. When Congress needs facts to determine whether existing laws are working and how they might be fixed, it often meets a Fifth Amendment stone wall. Congress can find the truth only if it gives witnesses sweeping immunity that then hinders the executive branch's prosecutorial function.

Thus, when Congress sought to investigate the Iran-contra scandal [sale of American arms to Iran in exchange for the release of American hostages, with a portion of the proceed going to fund anti-Communist rebels, or Contras, in Nicaragua] in 1987, it had to grant immunity to Oliver North in ways that ultimately led judges to overturn Mr. North's criminal conviction in 1989 for obstructing justice and other federal crimes. Although the evidence introduced against Mr. North was reliable, prosecutors could not prove that witnesses against him were not affected by his nationally televised Congressional testimony.

After that fiasco, Congress became cautious in its conduct of important investigations. When Congress sought to investi-

Mike Peters Editorial Cartoon is used with the permission of Grimmy, Inc. and the Cartoonist Group. All rights reserved.

gate campaign-finance abuses and possible Chinese influence in American politics in 1997, it chose not to force [chief fundraiser for the Democratic National Committee] John Huang to tell all he knew; such compelled testimony would have shielded Mr. Huang from criminal prosecution. Current Fifth Amendment doctrine thus prevents the legislature from doing its job of oversight and law reform.

President [George W.] Bush has urged strict construction of the Constitution, and the Fifth Amendment is a good place to start. Current case law ignores the Constitution's words, distorts constitutional structure and overprotects the guilty. But don't expect federal judges to alter this constitutional interpretation anytime soon. Enron executives are not the only ones who dislike confessing error.

> *"In many cases involving juvenile suspects, the custody analysis would be nonsensical absent some consideration of the suspect's age."*

Age Is Relevant in Determining the Applicability of the *Miranda* Rule

The Supreme Court's Decision

Sonia Sotomayor

In the following viewpoint, Sonia Sotomayor, writing for the majority of the US Supreme Court, argues that the age of a child subjected to police questioning is relevant to determining whether the child perceives to be in custody, and thus whether Miranda *warnings are required. Sotomayor claims that the court has long recognized the significance of a child's age for legal analysis. In this case, where a thirteen-year-old student was taken out of class and questioned at school, Sotomayor contends that it would be nonsensical to not consider age in determining whether the boy should have been informed of his* Miranda *rights. She concludes that age is relevant to the determination of whether or not a person can be considered to be subject to custodial interroga-*

Sonia Sotomayor, Majority Opinion, *J.D.B v. North Carolina*, US Supreme Court, June 16, 2011.

tion. Sotomayor has served as an associate justice of the Supreme Court since 2009.

This case presents the question whether the age of a child subjected to police questioning is relevant to the custody analysis of *Miranda v. Arizona* (1966). It is beyond dispute that children will often feel bound to submit to police questioning when an adult in the same circumstances would feel free to leave. Seeing no reason for police officers or courts to blind themselves to that commonsense reality, we hold that a child's age properly informs the *Miranda* custody analysis.

The Questioning of J.D.B.

Petitioner J.D.B. was a 13-year-old, seventh-grade student attending class at Smith Middle School in Chapel Hill, North Carolina when he was removed from his classroom by a uniformed police officer, escorted to a closed-door conference room, and questioned by police for at least half an hour.

This was the second time that police questioned J.D.B. in the span of a week. Five days earlier, two home break-ins occurred, and various items were stolen. Police stopped and questioned J.D.B. after he was seen behind a residence in the neighborhood where the crimes occurred. That same day, police also spoke to J.D.B.'s grandmother—his legal guardian—as well as his aunt.

Police later learned that a digital camera matching the description of one of the stolen items had been found at J.D.B.'s middle school and seen in J.D.B.'s possession. Investigator DiCostanzo, the juvenile investigator with the local police force who had been assigned to the case, went to the school to question J.D.B. Upon arrival, DiCostanzo informed the uniformed police officer on detail to the school (a so-called school resource officer), the assistant principal, and an administrative intern that he was there to question J.D.B. about the break-ins. Although DiCostanzo asked the school administrators to verify J.D.B.'s date of birth, address, and parent contact information from school records, neither the police officers nor the school administrators contacted J.D.B.'s grandmother.

The uniformed officer interrupted J.D.B.'s afternoon social studies class, removed J.D.B. from the classroom, and escorted him to a school conference room. There, J.D.B. was met by DiCostanzo, the assistant principal, and the administrative intern. The door to the conference room was closed. With the two police officers and the two administrators present, J.D.B. was questioned for the next 30 to 45 minutes. Prior to the commencement of questioning, J.D.B. was given neither *Miranda* warnings nor the opportunity to speak to his grandmother. Nor was he informed that he was free to leave the room.

The Confession of J.D.B.

Questioning began with small talk—discussion of sports and J.D.B.'s family life. DiCostanzo asked, and J.D.B. agreed, to discuss the events of the prior weekend. Denying any wrongdoing, J.D.B. explained that he had been in the neighborhood where the crimes occurred because he was seeking work mowing lawns. DiCostanzo pressed J.D.B. for additional detail about his efforts to obtain work; asked J.D.B. to explain a prior incident, when one of the victims returned home to find J.D.B. behind her house; and confronted J.D.B. with the stolen camera. The assistant principal urged J.D.B. to "do the right thing," warning J.D.B. that "the truth always comes out in the end."

Eventually, J.D.B. asked whether he would "still be in trouble" if he returned the "stuff." In response, DiCostanzo explained that return of the stolen items would be helpful, but "this thing is going to court" regardless. DiCostanzo then warned that he may need to seek a secure custody order if he believed that J.D.B. would continue to break into other homes. When J.D.B. asked what a secure custody order was, DiCostanzo explained that "it's where you get sent to juvenile detention before court."

After learning of the prospect of juvenile detention, J.D.B. confessed that he and a friend were responsible for the break-ins.

THE US SUPREME COURT ON THE RELEVANCE OF AGE

Age IS Relevant to the Custody Analysis of *Miranda v. Arizona* (1966)	Age IS NOT Relevant to the Custody Analysis of *Miranda v. Arizona* (1966)
Majority	**Dissent**
Justice Sonia Sotomayor (author of the majority opinion)	Justice Samuel Alito (author of the dissenting opinion)
Justice Anthony Kennedy	Chief Justice John Roberts
Justice Ruth Bader Ginsburg	Justice Antonin Scalia
Justice Stephen Breyer	Justice Clarence Thomas
Justice Elena Kagan	

Taken from: US Supreme Court, *J.D.B. v. North Carolina*, 2011.

DiCostanzo only then informed J.D.B. that he could refuse to answer the investigator's questions and that he was free to leave. Asked whether he understood, J.D.B. nodded and provided further detail, including information about the location of the stolen items. Eventually J.D.B. wrote a statement, at DiCostanzo's request. When the bell rang indicating the end of the school day, J.D.B. was allowed to leave to catch the bus home. . . .

The Coercive Nature of Police Interrogations

Any police interview of an individual suspected of a crime has "coercive aspects to it" [*Oregon v. Mathiason* (1977)]. Only those interrogations that occur while a suspect is in police custody, however, "heighte[n] the risk" that statements obtained are not the product of the suspect's free choice [*Dickerson v. United States* (2000)].

By its very nature, custodial police interrogation entails "inherently compelling pressures" [*Miranda*]. Even for an adult, the physical and psychological isolation of custodial interrogation can "undermine the individual's will to resist and . . . compel him to speak where he would not otherwise do so freely." Indeed, the pressure of custodial interrogation is so immense that it "can induce a frighteningly high percentage of people to confess to crimes they never committed" [*Corley v. United States* (2009)]. That risk is all the more troubling—and recent studies suggest, all the more acute—when the subject of custodial interrogation is a juvenile.

Recognizing that the inherently coercive nature of custodial interrogation "blurs the line between voluntary and involuntary statements" [*Dickerson*], this Court in *Miranda* adopted a set of prophylactic measures designed to safeguard the constitutional guarantee against self-incrimination. Prior to questioning, a suspect "must be warned that he has a right to remain silent, that any statement he does make may be used as evidence against him, and that he has a right to the presence of an attorney, either retained or appointed." And, if a suspect makes a statement during custodial interrogation, the burden is on the Government to show, as a "prerequisit[e]" to the statement's admissibility as evidence in the Government's case in chief, that the defendant "voluntarily, knowingly and intelligently" waived his rights.

The Custody Analysis

Because these measures protect the individual against the coercive nature of custodial interrogation, they are required "'only where there has been such a restriction on a person's freedom as to render him "in custody"'" [*Stansbury v. California* (1994) (quoting *Oregon v. Mathiason*)]. As we have repeatedly emphasized, whether a suspect is "in custody" is an objective inquiry.

> Two discrete inquiries are essential to the determination: first, what were the circumstances surrounding the interrogation; and second, given those circumstances, would a reasonable person have felt he or she was at liberty to terminate the in-

terrogation and leave. Once the scene is set and the players' lines and actions are reconstructed, the court must apply an objective test to resolve the ultimate inquiry: was there a formal arrest or restraint on freedom of movement of the degree associated with formal arrest. [*Thompson v. Keohane* (1995)].

Rather than demarcate a limited set of relevant circumstances, we have required police officers and courts to "examine all of the circumstances surrounding the interrogation" [*Stansbury*], including any circumstance that "would have affected how a reasonable person" in the suspect's position "would perceive his or her freedom to leave." On the other hand, the "subjective views harbored by either the interrogating officers or the person being questioned" are irrelevant. The test, in other words, involves no consideration of the "actual mindset" of the particular suspect subjected to police questioning [*Yarborough v. Alvarado* (2004)].

The benefit of the objective custody analysis is that it is "designed to give clear guidance to the police." Police must make in-the-moment judgments as to when to administer *Miranda* warnings. By limiting analysis to the objective circumstances of the interrogation, and asking how a reasonable person in the suspect's position would understand his freedom to terminate questioning and leave, the objective test avoids burdening police with the task of anticipating the idiosyncrasies of every individual suspect and divining how those particular traits affect each person's subjective state of mind.

The Relevance of Age

The State and its *amici* [supporters] contend that a child's age has no place in the custody analysis, no matter how young the child subjected to police questioning. We cannot agree. In some circumstances, a child's age "would have affected how a reasonable person" in the suspect's position "would perceive his or her freedom to leave" [*Stansbury*]. That is, a reasonable child subjected to police questioning will sometimes feel pressured to submit

In J.D.B. v. North Carolina *(2011), the US Supreme Court argued that juveniles are more likely to submit to police questioning without understanding their rights. The court ruled that age is a relevant factor in determining whether a person can be subject to custodial interrogation.* © Robert Nickelsberg/Getty Images.

when a reasonable adult would feel free to go. We think it clear that courts can account for that reality without doing any damage to the objective nature of the custody analysis.

A child's age is far "more than a chronological fact" [*Eddings v. Oklahoma* (1982)]. It is a fact that "generates common-sense conclusions about behavior and perception" [*Alvarado* (Justice Stephen Breyer dissenting)]. Such conclusions apply broadly to children as a class. And, they are self-evident to anyone who was a child once himself, including any police officer or judge.

Time and again, this Court has drawn these common-sense conclusions for itself. We have observed that children "generally are less mature and responsible than adults" [*Eddings*]; that they "often lack the experience, perspective, and judgment to recognize and avoid choices that could be detrimental to them" [*Bellotti v. Baird* (1979)]; that they "are more vulnerable or susceptible to . . . outside pressures" than adults [*Roper v. Simmons* (2005)]; and so on. Addressing the specific context of police interrogation, we have observed that events that "would leave a man cold and unimpressed can overawe and overwhelm a lad in his early teens" [*Haley v. Ohio* (1948)]. Describing no one child in particular, these observations restate what "any parent knows"—indeed, what any person knows—about children generally [*Roper*].

Our various statements to this effect are far from unique. The law has historically reflected the same assumption that children characteristically lack the capacity to exercise mature judgment and possess only an incomplete ability to understand the world around them. Like this Court's own generalizations, the legal disqualifications placed on children as a class—*e.g.*, limitations on their ability to alienate property, enter a binding contract enforceable against them, and marry without parental consent—exhibit the settled understanding that the differentiating characteristics of youth are universal. . . .

Age and the Custody Analysis

A child's age differs from other personal characteristics that, even when known to police, have no objectively discernible relationship to a reasonable person's understanding of his freedom of action. *Alvarado*, holds, for instance, that a suspect's prior interrogation history with law enforcement has no role to play in the custody analysis because such experience could just as easily lead a reasonable person to feel free to walk away as to feel compelled to stay in place. Because the effect in any given case would be "contingent [on the] psycholog[y]" of the individual suspect, the Court explained, such experience cannot be considered without compromising the objective nature of the custody analysis. A child's age, however, is different. Precisely because childhood yields objective conclusions like those we have drawn ourselves—among others, that children are "most susceptible to influence" [*Eddings*], and "outside pressures" [*Roper*],—considering age in the custody analysis in no way involves a determination of how youth "subjectively affect[s] the mindset" of any particular child.

In fact, in many cases involving juvenile suspects, the custody analysis would be nonsensical absent some consideration of the suspect's age. This case is a prime example. Were the court precluded from taking J. D. B.'s youth into account, it would be forced to evaluate the circumstances present here through the eyes of a reasonable person of average years. In other words, how would a reasonable adult understand his situation, after being removed from a seventh-grade social studies class by a uniformed school resource officer; being encouraged by his assistant principal to "do the right thing"; and being warned by a police investigator of the prospect of juvenile detention and separation from his guardian and primary caretaker? To describe such an inquiry is to demonstrate its absurdity. Neither officers nor courts can reasonably evaluate the effect of objective circumstances that, by their nature, are specific to children without accounting for the age of the child subjected to those circumstances.

Indeed, although the dissent suggests that concerns "regarding the application of the *Miranda* custody rule to minors can be accommodated by considering the unique circumstances present when minors are questioned in school," the effect of the schoolhouse setting cannot be disentangled from the identity of the person questioned. A student—whose presence at school is compulsory and whose disobedience at school is cause for disciplinary action—is in a far different position than, say, a parent volunteer on school grounds to chaperone an event, or an adult from the community on school grounds to attend a basketball game. Without asking whether the person "questioned in school" is a "minor," the coercive effect of the schoolhouse setting is unknowable. . . .

[W]e hold that so long as the child's age was known to the officer at the time of police questioning, or would have been objectively apparent to a reasonable officer, its inclusion in the custody analysis is consistent with the objective nature of that test. This is not to say that a child's age will be a determinative, or even a significant, factor in every case. It is, however, a reality that courts cannot simply ignore. . . .

The *Miranda* Rights of Children

Relying on our statements that the objective custody test is "designed to give clear guidance to the police" [*Alvarado*], the State . . . argues that a child's age must be excluded from the analysis in order to preserve clarity. Similarly, the dissent insists that the clarity of the custody analysis will be destroyed unless a "one-size-fits-all reasonable-person test" applies. In reality, however, ignoring a juvenile defendant's age will often make the inquiry more artificial, and thus only add confusion. And in any event, a child's age, when known or apparent, is hardly an obscure factor to assess. Though the State and the dissent worry about gradations among children of different ages, that concern cannot justify ignoring a child's age altogether. Just as police officers are competent to account for other objective circumstances that are a matter of degree such as the length of questioning or the number of officers present, so too are they competent to evaluate the effect of relative age. Indeed, they are competent to do so even though an interrogation room lacks the "reflective atmosphere of a [jury] deliberation room." The same is true of judges, including those whose childhoods have long since passed. In short, officers and judges need no imaginative powers, knowledge of developmental psychology, training in cognitive science, or expertise in social and cultural anthropology to account for a child's age. They simply need the common sense to know that a 7-year-old is not a 13-year-old and neither is an adult.

There is, however, an even more fundamental flaw with the State's plea for clarity and the dissent's singular focus on simplifying the analysis: Not once have we excluded from the custody analysis a circumstance that we determined was relevant and objective, simply to make the fault line between custodial and noncustodial "brighter." Indeed, were the guiding concern clarity and nothing else, the custody test would presumably ask only whether the suspect had been placed under formal arrest [*Berkemer v. McCarty* (1984)]. But we have rejected that "more easily administered line," recognizing that it would simply "enable the police to circumvent the constraints on custodial interrogations established by *Miranda*."

Finally, the State and the dissent suggest that excluding age from the custody analysis comes at no cost to juveniles' constitutional rights because the due process voluntariness test independently accounts for a child's youth. To be sure, that test permits consideration of a child's age, and it erects its own barrier to admission of a defendant's inculpatory statements at trial. But *Miranda*'s procedural safeguards exist precisely because the voluntariness test is an inadequate barrier when custodial interrogation is at stake. To hold, as the State requests, that a child's age is never relevant to whether a suspect has been taken into custody—and thus to ignore the very real differences between children and adults—would be to deny children the full scope of the procedural safeguards that *Miranda* guarantees to adults.

> *"Children and the mentally handicapped, or people whose recollections are clouded by drugs or alcohol, are particularly susceptible."*

Self-Incriminating Statements Are Sometimes False Confessions

Alexandra Perina

In the following viewpoint, Alexandra Perina argues that although a defendant's admission of guilt may seem like a good outcome to a trial, sometimes criminal suspects confess to crimes they did not commit. Perina claims that depending on the interrogation techniques used, at a certain point a false confession can be rational under a cost-benefit analysis. In particular, she claims that certain groups such as the young, the mentally handicapped, and the drug addicted are particularly susceptible to incriminating themselves for crimes for which they are not responsible. Perina is an attorney adviser in the US Department of State.

In criminal trials, a defendant's admission of guilt can trump even the proverbial smoking gun. A confession is the ideal civic solution: The perpetrator takes responsibility, and the public

Alexandra Perina, "'I Confess': Why Would an Innocent Person Profess Guilt," *Psychology Today*, March–April 2003. Copyright © 2003 by Psychology Today. All rights reserved. Reproduced by permission.

After delivering coerced confessions when they were teenagers, Raymond Santana (right), Kevin Richardson, and Yusef Salaam (left) were convicted in the 1989 Central Park rape case. They were vacated in 2002 and later sued the city of New York for wrongful imprisonment. © Frank Franklin II/AP Images.

sleeps soundly. But it's not always the end of the story. The convictions of five men who confessed to the 1989 rape and beating of a jogger in New York's Central Park were reversed after an imprisoned rapist took sole responsibility for the assault. Governor George Ryan commuted the sentences of Illinois' 150 death-row inmates to life in prison, due in part to concern about the role of false confessions in securing wrongful convictions.

Although it is difficult, if not impossible, to estimate the number of false confessions nationwide, a review of one decade's worth of murder cases in a single Illinois county found 247 instances in which the defendants' self-incriminating statements were thrown out by the court or found by a jury to be insufficiently convincing for conviction. (*The Chicago Tribune* conducted the investigation.)

Suspects with low IQs are particularly vulnerable to the pressures of police interrogation: They are less likely to understand the charges against them and the consequences of professing guilt. One of the suspects in the Central Park attack had an IQ of 87; another was aged 16 with a second-grade reading level.

But intelligence is by no means the decisive factor. Suspects with compliant or suggestible personalities and anxiety disorders may be hard-pressed to withstand an interrogation, according to Gisli Gudjonsson, Ph.D., a professor of forensic psychology at the Institute of Psychiatry in London. Gudjonsson's suggestibility scale is used by courts around the world to evaluate self-incriminating statements. But he cautions against seeking only personality-driven explanations for confessions: "A drug addict may not be particularly suggestible but may have a strong desire to get back out on the street."

Self-incriminating statements are often the result of a kind of cost-benefit analysis. "False confession is an escape hatch. It becomes rational under the circumstances," says Saul Kassin, Ph.D., a professor of psychology at Williams College in Massachusetts. The most common explanation given after the fact is that suspects "just wanted to go home."

This often indicates an inability to appreciate the consequences of a confession, a situation that police cultivate by communicating that a confession will be rewarded with lenient sentencing. Police may also offer mitigating factors—the crime was unintentional; the suspect was provoked.

The circumstances of interrogation are crucial. "Everybody has a breaking point. Nobody confesses falsely in an hour," says Kassin. The suspects in the Central Park case each spent between 14 and 30 hours under interrogation.

The use of false evidence (including statements such as, "Your fingerprints are on the gun") in interrogation is implicated in almost every false-confession case, but American courts have upheld the practice. This is not to say that police intentionally ensnare the innocent. Kassin notes that detectives are trained to believe they can make accurate judgments about a suspect's truthfulness, though "there's a level of overconfidence in the initial judgment, and they begin the interrogation with a presumption

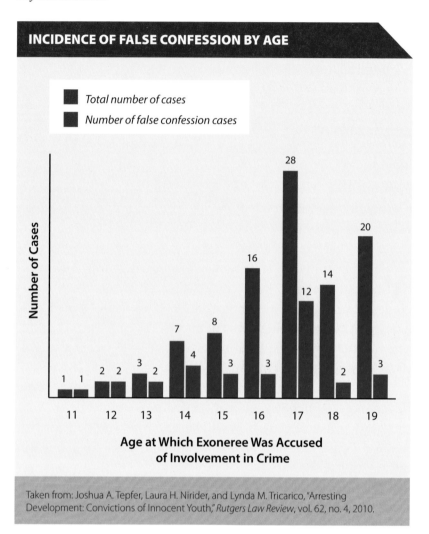

INCIDENCE OF FALSE CONFESSION BY AGE

■ Total number of cases
■ Number of false confession cases

Age at Which Exoneree Was Accused of Involvement in Crime

Number of Cases

Taken from: Joshua A. Tepfer, Laura H. Nirider, and Lynda M. Tricarico, "Arresting Development: Convictions of Innocent Youth," *Rutgers Law Review*, vol. 62, no. 4, 2010.

of guilt." Gudjonsson agrees: "Police officers need to know that they can elicit a false confession even if they don't intend to."

A particularly vulnerable defendant may begin to doubt his or her own memory when presented with false evidence. Children and the mentally handicapped, or people whose recollections are clouded by drugs or alcohol, are particularly susceptible. Interrogators may suggest that a suspect has repressed the memory. They then offer false evidence to fill in the gaps.

After intense interrogation, these suspects become sufficiently convinced of their own guilt and accept an "internalized" false confession.

False confessions are generated in cell blocks as well as interrogation rooms, a fact not lost on detectives under fire for the Central Park jogger case. One month after those convictions were vacated, a chagrined New York City Police Department issued its own revisionist theory: The inmate who claims he alone attacked the jogger may have falsely confessed due to threats from other inmates or the desire to transfer to another prison.

> "Continuous questioning of a suspect
> who has essentially exercised his right
> to silence for almost three hours . . .
> seems like coercion to me."

The Right to Remain Silent Is Increasingly Threatened

Craig M. Bradley

In the following viewpoint, Craig M. Bradley argues that the US Supreme Court's decision in Berghuis v. Thompkins *(2010) threatens the right guaranteed under* Miranda v. Arizona *(1966) to remain silent when interrogated by law enforcement. Bradley contends that the court erred in concluding that a criminal suspect who does not explicitly assert his right to remain silent but remains silent for hours may continue to be interrogated. Bradley claims that continued interrogation runs the risk of becoming coercive and that silence in response to questioning should cause the interrogation to cease after a reasonable time period. Bradley is the Robert A. Lucas Chair of Law at the Indiana University Maurer School of Law.*

Ever since Warren Burger was sworn in as chief justice of the Supreme Court in 1969, *Miranda v. Arizona* [1966] has been a favorite target of the predominantly conservative Court, which

Craig M. Bradley, "Squeezing Miranda," *Trial*, October 2010, pp. 52, 54. Copyright © 2010 by Craig M. Bradley. All rights reserved. Reproduced by permission.

has limited, distinguished, or ignored it in repeated decisions. *Berghuis v. Thompkins* [2010] is a particularly striking example of this trend.

Examining the Right to Remain Silent

Thompkins dealt with the right to remain silent. The defendant, Van Chester Thompkins, was attested for murder and given his *Miranda* warnings. There is no question that he understood them, although he declined to sign a form acknowledging this. He remained silent during a three-hour interrogation but said "yes" when the police asked at the end of their questioning whether he prayed to God for forgiveness for killing the victim.

Thompkins's motion to suppress this statement was denied at trial, but on appeal from denial of federal *habeas corpus* relief, the Sixth Circuit ruled in his favor. The appeals court found that Thompkins's "persistent silence for nearly three hours" during questioning sent a "clear and unequivocal message" that he did not wish to waive his *Miranda* rights.

The court acknowledged that the 1979 Supreme Court decision in *North Carolina v. Butler* [1979] established that waiver could be implied from a suspect's conduct after he or she received *Miranda* warnings. But that decision also reiterated *Miranda*'s admonition that "a valid waiver will not be presumed simply from the silence of the accused after warnings are given or simply from the fact that a confession was in fact eventually obtained."

While an implied waiver of *Miranda* rights could be found when a suspect talked freely to police after receiving warnings, the Sixth Circuit found, a suspect like Thompkins, who showed no inclination to talk during his interrogation, could not be held to have impliedly waived his rights.

The US Supreme Court's Decision in *Thompkins*

The Supreme Court, in an opinion written by Justice Anthony Kennedy and supported by four other justices, reversed. The majority admitted that according to *Miranda*, "a heavy burden rests on the government to demonstrate that the defendant knowingly and intelligently waived his privilege." But "the main purpose of *Miranda* is to ensure that an accused is advised of and understands the right to remain silent and the right to counsel," the Court said, citing a previous finding that "our subsequent cases have reduced the impact of the *Miranda* rule on legitimate law enforcement while reaffirming the decision's core ruling that unwarned statements may not be used as evidence in the prosecution's case in chief."

Suspects must invoke their right to remain silent unambiguously, the Court ruled, and Thompkins did not tell the interrogators that he wanted to remain silent. He also impliedly waived this right by choosing to speak, the Court held, and it is irrelevant that he stayed quiet for almost three hours after receiving a *Miranda* warning.

In so holding, the Court redefined what the "core" of *Miranda* is and ignored its "heavy burden" language. To hold that the right to remain silent can be waived by a suspect who steadfastly refuses to speak in the face of accusations is inconsistent with any realistic notion of voluntary waiver. Now, the burden is on the suspect to say that he or she wants "to remain silent or that he [or she does] not want to talk to the police." The language of *Miranda* has been rendered inoperative.

The Dissenting Opinion in *Thompkins*

The dissent, written by Justice Sonia Sotomayor and joined by three others, agreed that the police need not attempt to get an explicit waiver from every suspect—the implied waiver approved in *Butler* is acceptable. But, Sotomayor noted, the majority would require too much of suspects who want to preserve their right to remain silent:

> The Court concludes today that a criminal suspect waives his right to remain silent if, after sitting tacit and uncommunica-

The Supreme Court's Holding in
Berghuis v. Thompkins

A suspect who has received and understood the *Miranda* warnings, and has not invoked his *Miranda* rights, waives the right to remain silent by making an uncoerced statement to the police. Thompkins did not invoke his right to remain silent and stop the questioning. Understanding his rights in full, he waived his right to remain silent by making a voluntary statement to the police. The police, moreover, were not required to obtain a waiver of Thompkins's right to remain silent before interrogating him.

Anthony Kennedy, Majority Opinion, Berghuis v. Thompkins, *US Supreme Court, vol. 560, June 1, 2010.*

tive through nearly three hours of police interrogation, he utters a few one-word responses. The Court also concludes that a suspect who wishes to guard his right to remain silent against such a finding of "waiver" must, counterintuitively, speak— and must do so with sufficient precision to satisfy a clear-statement rule that construes ambiguity in favor of the police.

Sotomayor found that the majority holding was flatly inconsistent with both *Miranda* and *Butler* and created a new general principal of law. Of course, *Miranda* is not holy writ and is only loosely based on the Fifth Amendment. If a majority of the Court, some 44 years later, wants to change it, it can, although it would be refreshing if it would admit that it was doing so.

The Future Impact of the Court's Ruling

Thompkins establishes a relatively clear rule: Silence is not enough to cease an interrogation. If the Court had held otherwise, it

The US Supreme Court has ruled that a suspect must specifically invoke their right to remain silent or an interrogation may continue. © Fisun Ivan/Shutterstock.

would have given rise to the question of how much silence is enough. Could the police continue to question a suspect for five minutes? Ten minutes? Surely some questioning would have to be allowed in order to determine if a suspect, not having explicitly waived his or her rights, would be cooperative enough to establish an implied waiver.

Despite clarity on that issue, we are now faced with the question of what a suspect must say to invoke his or her rights. Certainly, placing the burden on suspects to immediately and unambiguously express their assertion of rights is helpful to police. But must the accused make one of the two statements officially approved by the Court—that he or she wants to remain silent or does not want to talk to the police? What if the suspect says, "I don't have anything to say"? Presumably, a mere expression of doubt, such as "I'm not sure it's a good idea to talk to you," will not be enough.

Given that many suspects are intimidated by the interrogation environment, it will not be unusual for them to fail to be definitive in their assertion of rights. But it seems the majority would say, "We don't care. We allow police to use deceit, to make religious appeals, and to question suspects for extended periods as long as their tactics don't undercut our rather loose standards for voluntariness."

This decision seems to shed some light on another issue—when questioning can resume after an assertion of the right to silence. In *Edwards v. Arizona* [1981] and *Michigan v. Mosley* [1975], the Court held that assertions of the right to counsel and the right to remain silent are different. An invocation of the right to counsel ceases an interrogation, but *Mosley* held that when the right to remain silent is asserted, interrogation can resume under certain circumstances. That case involved subsequent questioning at a different time by different police about an unrelated crime after a new warning was given.

In *Thompkins*, the Court held that there is no reason to adopt different standards for determining when an accused has invoked the right to counsel or the right to remain silent. "Both protect the privilege against compulsory self-incrimination by requiring an interrogation to cease when either right is invoked," the Court noted.

This implies that when the right to silence is unambiguously asserted, questioning must cease, at least as to the instant case. And it suggests that *Mosley*—which is different, as the issue is when an invocation of rights may be overridden—is limited to questioning about a different crime at a different time.

When Questioning Becomes Coercion

In the end, I disagree with the majority because of the unusual facts of this case, leaving aside the inconsistency with *Miranda*. Continuous questioning of a suspect who has essentially exercised his right to silence for almost three hours—unlike the suspects in previous cases, who talked freely—seems like coercion to me. Thompkins's failure to say the magic words "counsel" or "silence" doesn't make his eventual capitulation to a religious appeal voluntary.

I would have held that the police can question someone who declines to explicitly waive his or her right to silence for five minutes, after which they must conclude that a voluntary implied waiver will not be forthcoming.

Organizations to Contact

The editors have compiled the following list of organizations concerned with the issues debated in this book. The descriptions are derived from materials provided by the organizations. All have publications or information available for interested readers. The list was compiled on the date of publication of the present volume; the information provided here may change. Be aware that many organizations take several weeks or longer to respond to inquiries, so allow as much time as possible.

American Bar Association (ABA)

740 15th Street NW
Washington, DC 20005-1019
(202) 662-1000 • fax: (202) 662-1501
email: crimjustice@abanet.org
website: www.abanet.org

The American Bar Association is a voluntary membership organization for professionals within the legal field that provides law school accreditation and works to promote justice, excellence of those within the legal profession, and respect for the law. The Section of Individual Rights and Responsibilities of the ABA is dedicated to addressing civil rights and civil liberties issues and ensuring that protection of individual rights remains a focus of legal and policy decisions. This section of the ABA publishes *Human Rights,* a quarterly magazine, and also makes available its *amicus curiae* briefs on behalf of parties before the courts in cases involving individual liberties.

American Center for Law and Justice (ACLJ)

PO Box 90555
Washington, DC 20090-0555
(800) 296-4529
website: www.aclj.org

The American Center for Law and Justice is dedicated to protecting religious and constitutional freedoms. ACLJ has participated in numerous cases before the US Supreme Court, Federal Court of Appeals, Federal District Courts, and various state courts regarding freedom of religion and freedom of speech. ACLJ has numerous position papers and radio show episodes available on its website, including, "Students' Rights."

American Civil Liberties Union (ACLU)

125 Broad Street, 18th Floor
New York, NY 10004
(212) 549-2500
email: infoaclu@aclu.org
website: www.aclu.org

The American Civil Liberties Union is a national organization that works to defend Americans' civil rights as guaranteed in the US Constitution. The ACLU works in courts, legislatures, and communities to defend First Amendment rights, the right to equal protection, the right to due process, and the right to privacy. The ACLU publishes the semiannual newsletter *Civil Liberties Alert* as well as articles such as "The First and Fifth Amendments Are Not Optional."

Campaign for Youth Justice (CFYJ)

1012 14th Street NW, Suite 610
Washington, DC 20005
(202) 558-3580 • fax: (202) 386-9807
email: info@cfyj.org
website: www.campaignforyouthjustice.org

The Campaign for Youth Justice is dedicated to ending the practice of trying, sentencing, and incarcerating youth under eighteen in the adult criminal justice system. CFYJ advocates for juvenile justice reform through providing support to federal, state, and local campaigns; coordinating outreach to parents, youth, and families;

fostering national coalition-building; encouraging media relations; conducting research; and publishing reports and advocacy materials. Among its numerous publications is the national report, "You're An Adult Now: Youth in Adult Criminal Justice Systems."

Center for Public Education

1680 Duke Street
Alexandria, VA 22314
(703) 838-6722 • fax (703) 548-5613
website: www.centerforpubliceducation.org
email: centerforpubliced@nsba.org

The Center for Public Education is a resource center set up by the National School Boards Association. The Center for Public Education works to provide information about public education, leading to more understanding about our schools, more communitywide involvement, and better decision making by school leaders on behalf of all students in their classrooms. Among the many articles available on the center's website is "Search and Seizure, Due Process, and Public Schools."

Coalition for Juvenile Justice (CJJ)

1319 F Street NW, Suite 402
Washington, DC 20004
(202) 467-0864 • fax: (202) 887-0738
email: info@juvjustice.org
website: www.juvjustice.org

The Coalition for Juvenile Justice is dedicated to preventing children and youth from becoming involved in the courts and upholding the highest standards of care when youth enter the justice system. CJJ promotes evidence-informed policies and practices in delinquency reduction and prevention and works for juvenile justice system reforms that improve fairness. Among the resources available on the CJJ's website is the paper, "Conditions of Confinement for Young Offenders."

National Education Association (NEA)

1201 16th Street NW
Washington, DC 20036-3290
(202) 833-4000 • fax (202) 822-7974
website: www.nea.org

The National Education Association is an educator membership organization that works to advance the rights of educators and children. The NEA focuses its energy on improving the quality of teaching, increasing student achievement, and making schools safe places to learn. Among the magazines that the NEA publishes are *NEA Today* and *Thought & Action.*

National Institute of Justice (NIJ)

810 7th Street NW
Washington, DC 20531
(202) 307-2942
website: www.nij.gov

The National Institute of Justice, a component of the Office of Justice Programs, US Department of Justice, is dedicated to improving knowledge and understanding of crime and justice issues through science. NIJ provides objective and independent knowledge and tools to reduce crime and promote justice, particularly at the state and local levels. NIJ publishes the monthly *NIJ Journal*, available at its website, which includes such recent articles as "Managing Gangs in Schools."

National Youth Rights Association (NYRA)

1101 15th Street NW, Suite 200
Washington, DC 20005
(202) 835-1739
website: www.youthrights.org

The National Youth Rights Association is a youth-led national nonprofit organization dedicated to fighting for the civil rights and liberties of young people. NYRA has more than seven thousand members representing all fifty states. It seeks to lower the voting age, lower the drinking age, repeal curfew laws, and protect student rights.

Office of Juvenile Justice and Delinquency Prevention (OJJDP)

810 7th Street NW
Washington, DC 20531
(202) 307-5911
website: ojjdp.ncjrs.org

The Office of Juvenile Justice and Delinquency Prevention, a component of the Office of Justice Programs, US Department of Justice, collaborates with professionals from diverse disciplines to improve juvenile justice policies and practices. OJJDP accomplishes its mission by supporting states, local communities, and tribal jurisdictions in their efforts to develop and implement effective programs for juveniles. Through its Juvenile Justice Clearinghouse, OJJDP provides access to fact sheets, summaries, reports, and articles from its journal, *Juvenile Justice.*

For Further Reading

Books

Corona Brezina, *The Fifth Amendment: Double Jeopardy, Self-Incrimination, and Due Process of Law.* New York: Rosen, 2011.

Jennifer Chacón, *Criminal Procedure: The Fifth Amendment: Its Constitutional History and the Contemporary Debate.* New York: Prometheus, 2011.

Michael D. Cicchini, *Tried and Convicted: How Police, Prosecutors, and Judges Destroy Our Constitutional Rights.* Lanham, MD: Rowman and Littlefield, 2012.

Alan M. Dershowitz, *Is There a Right to Remain Silent?: Coercive Interrogation and the Fifth Amendment After 9/11.* New York: Oxford University Press, 2008.

Alan M. Goldstein and Naomi E. Sevin Goldstein, *Evaluating Capacity to Waive Miranda Rights.* New York: Oxford University Press, 2010.

Nancy Jessica Holmes and Catherine Ramen, *Understanding the Rights of the Accused.* New York: Rosen, 2012.

Thomas A. Jacobs, *Teens Take It to Court: Young People Who Challenged the Law—And Changed Your Life.* Minneapolis, MN: Free Spirit, 2006.

G.S. Prentzas, *Miranda Rights: Protecting the Rights of the Accused.* New York: Rosen, 2006.

Paul Ruschmann, *Miranda Rights.* New York: Chelsea House, 2007.

Steven M. Salky, *The Privilege of Silence: Fifth Amendment Protections Against Self-Incrimination.* Chicago: American Bar Association, 2009.

Louis Michael Seidman, *Silence and Freedom.* Stanford, CA: Stanford Law and Politics, 2007.

Randy Singer, *Self-Incrimination.* Carol Stream, IL: Tyndale House, 2010.

Gary L. Stuart, *Miranda: The Story of America's Right to Remain Silent.* Tucson: University of Arizona Press, 2008.

Rob Warden and Steven A. Drizin, eds., *True Stories of False Confessions.* Evanston, IL: Northwestern University Press, 2009.

Periodicals and Internet Sources

Paul G. Cassell, "Take Technicality Out of *Miranda*," *Los Angeles Times*, December 6, 1999.

Paul G. Cassell, "The Paths Not Taken: The Supreme Court's Failures in *Dickerson*," *Michigan Law Review*, March 2001.

James J. Duane, "The Right to Remain Silent: A New Answer to an Old Question," *Criminal Justice*, Summer 2010.

Nicole J. Ettlinger, "Note: You Have the Right to Remain Thirteen: Considering Age in Juvenile Interrogations in *J.D.B. v. North Carolina*," *Buffalo Law Review*, April 2012.

Hillary B. Farber, "The Role of the Parent/Guardian in Juvenile Custodial Interrogations: Friend or Foe?," *American Criminal Law Review*, Summer 2004.

Martin Guggenheim and Randy Hertz, "*J.D.B.* and the Maturing of Juvenile Confession Suppression Law," *Washington University Journal of Law and Policy*, Winter 2012.

Kenneth J. King, "Waiving Childhood Goodbye: How Juvenile Courts Fail to Protect Children from Unknowing, Unintelligent, and Involuntary Waivers of *Miranda* Rights," *Wisconsin Law Review*, 2006.

Kit Kinports, "The Supreme Court's Love-Hate Relationship with *Miranda*," *Journal of Criminal Law and Criminology*, Spring 2011.

Charles Krauthammer, "Supreme Hypocrisy," *Washington Post*, June 30, 2000.

Marsha Levick, "*J.D.B. v. North Carolina*: The US Supreme Court Heralds the Emergence of the 'Reasonable Juvenile' in American Criminal Law," *Criminal Law Reporter*, August 24, 2011.

Dahlia Lithwick, "Read Me a Story, and My Rights," *Slate*, June 16, 2011. www.slate.com.

"*Miranda* Rights for Middle Schoolers: A Juvenile Suspect's Age Deserves Consideration Under Rules for Police Interrogations," *New York Times*, June 17, 2011.

Meg Penrose, "*Miranda*, Please Report to the Principal's Office," *Fordham Urban Law Journal*, March 2006.

Lourdes M. Rosado, "Outside the Police Station: Dealing with the Potential for Self-Incrimination in Juvenile Court," *Washington University Journal of Law and Policy*, Winter 2012.

Jeffrey Rosen, "*Miranda* Critics Use 'Alice in Wonderland' Logic," *Politico*, February 16, 2010. www.politico.com.

Jeffrey Rosen, "Right Should Remain Silent: Don't End '*Miranda*.' Mend It," *New Republic*, May 1, 2000.

Jonathan L. Rudd, "You Have to Speak Up to Remain Silent: The Supreme Court Revisits the *Miranda* Right to Silence," *FBI Law Enforcement Bulletin*, September 2010.

"Speak for Silence," *The Record* (Bergen County, NJ), June 6, 2010.

Index